Iyanla Bivinet Ashi Au Bari is a Master Shamanic Healer and Teacher of Core Andean Practices. She offers healing to open the doors of possibility for her global clients. She is the author of *Living Shamanism, Unveiling the Mystery & the Sacred Divine Mothers (Iyami)*. She is also a contributing author to *Shamanic Transformation, The True Stories of Awakening & What Is Shamanism*.

She has studied with teachers and mystics from both the Andean Qero and Aymara Traditions and West African Orisha traditions. She is also studying Quareia High Magic. She constantly seeks the Path of Purity and Truth. As a child and kin of the Divine Mothers Iyami, she works from the Inner core of the Mothers, working with injustice to help restore balance to the Earth. She works with conflict resolution, karmic issues and clearing negative dark forces. She is a conduit for alchemical change and transformation.

About the Counsel and Contributor

Chrystalle Ariel is a Hereditary Metaphysician and an Initiate of The Holy Mysteries. She is a Record Keeper and Sacred Scribe of several spiritual lineages. A trained broadcast journalist and metaphysical counsellor, she was born into the Lineage of the Orishas and the Divine Mothers in West Africa. She is steeped in the Mysteries of Cosmic Luminosities, The Mills of the Gods and the Infinite began to grind in early life. This allowed for Multidimensional living that initially brought elation and then many tests, learning to straddle the inner and outer realms of light and creation. She works with many Divine Allies. This allows her to navigate life deeply in sacred service on earth at this pivotal time. She does this from an ever-expanding place of Truth, Freedom and Evolution.

Chrystalle is available for In-Depth Metaphysical Readings, Hand Analysis (Chiromancy), Lifepath Maps, Bush Flower Remedies/ Readings, and Herbal/Nutritional Healing.

I would like to make some special dedications and thanks to those who love, guide and counsel me; these unique souls have not only agreed and signed up to be around and support me in this current paradigm, but their presence and never-ending support mean the world to me personally and for my purpose.

First and foremost, I want to thank my beloveds. My husband, Paul, who agreed to partner me along the continual rollercoaster of life and who is always on hand to love and support me unconditionally. My dear daughters, Ella and Katie, who are my joy and who I hold so dearly in my heart centre and who have become my most excellent teachers.

Chrystalle K. Arial, if not for you, this door would not have opened to connect me with my lineage (Iyami – Divine Mothers) once again, and I thank you for always being there to unravel my questions and to support this journey.

Last but not least, to those who walk beside me on this voyage of the sacred quest and provide such great laughter with their constant willingness to do the work we are here to do. You are indeed the steady, peaceful, amazing warriors of the Path of Purity and Truth.

Iyanla Bivinet-Ashi Au Bari

THE SACRED DIVINE MOTHERS (IYAMI)

Revered Counsel and Keepers of Ancient Sacred Wisdom

AUSTIN MACAULEY PUBLISHERS™

LONDON • CAMBRIDGE • NEW YORK • SHARJAH

A CIP catalogue record for this title is available from the British Library.

ISBN 9781398445123 (Paperback)
ISBN 9781398445130 (ePub e-book)

www.austinmacauley.com

First Published 2023
Austin Macauley Publishers Ltd®
1 Canada Square
Canary Wharf
London
E14 5AA

It is with honour and great respect that I acknowledge the keepers of the Traditions of IFA/Orisha both in their homelands of West Africa and the Diasporas.

Particularly I would like to acknowledge Chrystalle K. Ariel and her substantial abilities to help bring this work to the world. Dr Ayele Kumari (Chief Abiye Tayese) for her extensive knowledge of the traditions of IFA/Orisha/Iyami and her wonderful classes. Iyanifa Vassa Olufadeke of the IFA Foundation, who first began my knowledge and training. Lastly, Mama Zogbe Mamaissii Vivian Hunter-Hindrew of mamiwata.com and her incredible books opened doors beyond my imagination to the history and etymology of West Africa.

Table of Contents

Introduction

The idea, or should I say the urging, to write this book, came from 'Iyami, The Divine Mothers'. You will hear me refer to them many times throughout this book, and I will explain later who they are. For now, I would like to clarify the energy behind the urging.

I first met them three years before I began writing this. It was in August 2016; I had booked an appointment with a renowned, Metaohysical Seer and Counsel. How this meeting came about was also serendipitous. The story begins a year before this. I was busy seeing clients regularly. As they say, things come in threes. , I had booked appointments for three clients, from different locations around Ireland.

Sometimes, in a session I ask how my clients have come to hear about me, each one, stated that 'Chrystalle', had sent them. It was only after the third client expressed where he had come from, I asked, "I know this is strange, but who is this Chrystalle?"

He explained who Chrystalle was and what she did. During his explanation, I recognised her description. I asked if there was another name she was known? He replied yes and then I remembered where I had met 'Chrystalle' before. It was twenty years ago when my husband and I were training in Andean Shamanism, with Dr Alberto Villoldo here in Ireland. I remembered her very well; we hadn't ever spoken, this, of course, isn't unusual as the classes often contained around 70 people, who had come from all over the world to train. We too had come over from the UK to take part in the training. When I last saw Chrystalle, we were living in the UK, without any plans of moving to Ireland.

After I had finished with this particular client, I was puzzled to understand why Chrystalle was referring clients to me; after all, it was not as if we moved in the same circles.

A few weeks later, my husband was struggling with an issue that threw out some challenges in his life and he couldn't see a way forward. I remembered how Chrystalle worked, and I discussed her gifts with him. He thought it would be a great idea to have an appointment with her. When the day of his appointment arrived, we left our home to start the hour-long journey. We had the directions and a map, but somehow along the way, we got lost in the mountains of Tipperary. It was an extraordinary and stressful journey. Finally, we arrived at our destination, a tiny village in rural Tipperary. My husband went to his appointment and came out about 2 hours later. I could tell by his face, he was in shock, especially when all he could say was 'Wow'. Now, my husband isn't easily impressed, especially with those who do any medium type work, let alone with seers. With Chrystalle, it was different, he came out clutching his tape, we said our goodbyes and began the journey home. Again, taking a completely different route from the way we came. Throughout the car journey, He was chatting away, animately recounting what had happened and what Chrystalle had told him.

The very next day, I listened to his tape. I remember thinking to myself; this is tremendously evolved. I excitedly made an appointment for myself about three months later.

When the day arrived, I was excited, but a little worried about what I would hear, especially if she were to tell me about my life's purpose. You see, I have been a Shaman healer, Teacher and Author for over ten years. I remembered thinking that morning in the shower, "What if I am not meant to do this at all, or what if the Guardian Spirits think I'm a fraud?"

As these negative thoughts ran through my head, the fear and doubt urged me to adopt a cynical mindset. "I know," I thought, "I'm going to test her ability." With this thought running rampant, I spoke aloud two questions, the first, 'how many dimensions are there really in existence?' and two, 'what will happen with my Mum's illness?' I continued to get ready, and we set off, of course, the route we took was again completely different from the last time.

We arrived at the location, the same time as Chrystalles secretary who informed us Chrystalle had been delayed because she had experienced an unusually tricky morning.

We waited inside for about half an hour when all of a sudden a car pulled up and Chrystalle came inside the house, looking very flustered. My husband said hello, and I walked forward to hug her. Chrystalle hurriedly rushed past me, saying, "I have to go and get ready." All of a sudden, I was lost in my head again, as my ego informed me this was surely going to be a problematic appointment for me!

Finally, I was called in as Chrystalle was ready; she apologised to me and explained what had happened. "Julie, I am very sorry for the delay, but when I was at home I experienced a very strong energy from 'The Mothers', I had to keep sitting down." I was sat there thinking, "Oh my goodness, who are these 'Mothers'?" Chrystalle went on to explain; she had never experienced such a persistent visit from these extraordinary beings before, especially here in Ireland. Even as she was talking to me, they were urging her to begin the session.

That day was my first introduction to 'The Divine Mothers', or Iyami to share their actual title. From this moment in time, I knew my life, and my work would change and become enhanced into a deeper and more focussed way of working, and little did I realise how different it would become. The information, she shared and explained to me during the afternoon, was confusing, yet I knew I had to surrender to her counsel. I also knew I had received information that was so ancient and profound, my western mind, was indeed going to need some time to process it all. One thing Chrystalle repeated throughout the session was, "I know this is a lot to take in." Well, she wasn't kidding, as it took me the best part of a year and a half, merely to begin to put it all into practice. For once in my life, I could not rely on being taught by a physical book or a known teacher. Far from it, everything shared, guided and even initiated, comes from other dimensions, straight into me in reality and during my dream time. Even, the need to write this book came to me from the higher realms, the title of the book, itself was illuminated in the quietness of a visualisation, along with a fervent desire to begin writing it.

By the way, remember the two questions I boldly asked in the shower before my session? Well, Chrystalle answered them within ten minutes of our meeting, when she said: "Well, you know, there are many more dimensions than we know about, there are at least 22 in the centre of the Earth, alone." As my eyebrows raised ever so slightly, I was thinking, "Oh my goodness, they heard me." Then nearer the end of my session, she pointed to one of the unusual-looking cards I had pulled earlier and said: "What's wrong with your Mums health?" Finally, I thought to myself; there you go you doubting Thomas, your test was heard, do not be suspicious any longer, it's time to get to work.

Preface

The very idea of life beyond what is considered a now standard archaic patriarchal view is possibly lesser-known and un-acknowledged. The implication of a once-powerful feminine force of Creator Goddesses and Priestesses, having held status and prominence and who had dominion over the Ancient World is for many unthinkable. The latter more commonly recognised as the famous Oracles and Seers, who guided the High Kings and Men of influence throughout the ancient lands. Indeed, they held power and position in the Ancient World. They served no masculine figurehead or God; instead, they served a pantheon of powerful deities, a force of immense reckoning beyond the veils of reality and form. These Priestesses were known as the Serpent worshippers; they hailed from ambiguity and the higher hidden worlds. These women kept the secrets of where we came from and who seeded us here on Earth. Their daily ritual was imbued with honouring and appeasing these Deities and ensuring their bidding was carried out in the realms of man. Beyond the Deities, sent here as ambassadors to help humankind from 'Father God' himself is better known throughout the tribal cultures of Earth. Yet what do we know about the Divine Mothers, Iyami who birthed us all?

There is, of course, a known biological fact, all living female species (whether human or animal, unless of course, you are a seahorse), create life inside their wombs using the precious masculine seed. If you are like me, you may have pondered how the first humans arrived here on Earth? And consequently who was the second and the third who came after that? Whose belly did the first human birth come out of?

There are, after all, many unanswered questions.

Of course, science and Darwinists have their views. And the Bible scriptures provide us with a template view of a Primordial Adam and Eve. The evidence is there, except for a clear and concise translation. Our minds create reality, built on a library set of beliefs and opinions. Therefore one man's idea isn't the same as another. What does interest me, lies in a vast pool of hidden truths and knowledge about our source induction here on Earth. The strange and biased Worldview of history seems to collude with the wishes of Monarchy and Religious Hierarchies insistence of cataloging what happened by way of a manipulated conjecture.

It is rare to actualise facts when the time has long gone and has been placed in the vaults underneath libraries, the Vatican and Museums. Every piece of knowledge having predated a colluded way of life has become secreted into a misrepresented or inside fairytale annuals of mythology. Where other existences or the idea of other lifeforms, are excommunicated into a fantasmagorical place of conjecture. When you examine such a worldview from its biased position of records, one has to question. Why so much has been ignored rather than celebrated as part of humanities rich tapestry of evolution. Perhaps it is because it all happened so long ago, far beyond man's ability to remember or even record. After all, there is such a limited amount of evidence available which can explain or back up these ideologies. Let's face it, so many records and important scrolls were destroyed along the way. Even the Bible itself had much of its essential content omitted and disregarded. Perhaps by accident or perhaps by deliberate and intelligent omission, carried out by those who feel we should never know the truth.

Today, when anyone offers a difference in constructive opinion, a possibility of something Science hasn't a proven theory for yet. It is often downgraded to a conspiracy theory or demeaned as 'new age or hippy', ways of seeing the world. Laughed off as having been written by someone who is clearly on the 'wacky baccy' or who lives with their head in the clouds.

For me, silence can no longer be the norm, as research has to take precedence as the journey into understanding my lineages and previous lifetimes, must now become the pillars of what happened and how humanity evolved towards its state of patriarchal dominance. And it has to be served on a golden platter with a caveat to be shared.

The main contributors and research in writing about 'The Sacred Divine Mothers (Iyami)', comes originally from the African tradition, where Iyami, first showed up and during the hundreds of thousands of years following, they have been revered, feared, worshipped, adored and denied.

In Africa today, there are still, many groups claiming to uphold these core beliefs, and there are also many who have reformed and hijacked the core teachings using a somewhat sketchy, artistic licence in its reformation in their worship and rituals. Claiming to come from a reliable source, it is sad to say, there are those, who have taken a mere part of the original and sacred teachings and used them merely to gain power and status. These people are indeed delusional and often money driven.

However, there always has to be an original early 'religion' who venerated and adored 'Iyami', wherein, the teachings and truth come directly from Source, these have been found in the Mami Wata, Yeveh and Vodoun Religions.

Mami Wata is celebrated as being the Divine original truth and wisdom guide, Yeveh incorporates ancestral worship, and Voudon came from the Serpent Deities. (Voudon, is the pure form of the later embellished Voodoo) These three fragments of the whole are drawn from a profound cosmology, ritual ceremony and philosophy. One whose culture spreads over 300,000 years and of which the art of divination underpins its very core, known initially as AFA, now more commonly known as IFA a name generated from the Yoruba traditions, native to Benin, Togo and Nigeria of West Africa.

'We Are'

We are from the centre of Earths deepest Cosmogony.
Our bloodline is pure with unabashed progeny.
We are the deepness of Sacred Law and Mystery.
Though much of our existence has been wiped from history.
We were present from the beginning of humanity.
Our life force was misappropriated and labelled by profanity.
Our powers held the status and our abilities respected.
Our Priestesses honoured and deeply connected.
These were Alchemists and Counsel, Healers and Seers.
Their protectors were loyal and fierce Amazonian buccaneers.
Kings asked my Priestesses for guidance, magic and audience.
Kings never needed to be assured of our credentials.
'We are' the Divine Ancestral Mothers.
Our realms originate in the Earth, in Fire, Air and its Waters.
We need no permission or trivial enticing.
We do not need your recognition or obvious soothing.
As we are, the Mothers of Earths initial creation.
We come back to bring harmony to your imbalanced nations.
We remain the powers of Creation and counsel from the ether.
We exist outside of humanities scope of law, rule and tether.
We remain connected to the children of our lineage.
We reside both in the Eden and within the belly of Earth.
Poised in silence with patience, awaiting humanities rebirth.
We are the architects and creators who will rebuild the rainbow
bridge.

Chapter 1
Her Story Lost

The Divine Providence of Mami Wata

[1]The manifestation of the original and natural order as will through the divine Logos. Responsible for establishing human societies, moral law, religious institutions and sacred authority, for maintaining order on Earth.

Vivian Hunter-Hindrew M.ED, Chief Hounon Amengansie

In the main, and it is safe to say, we have a narrow worldview when we talk about history. In itself, history is often punctuated by religious knowledge, because it was often the Monks who penned what happened. History ushers understanding of where we came from and what happened to humanity through a condensed age. And we can determine certain datelines and events throughout human history because we assume the escapades of humanity is an exact account in its history annals. Indeed the scribes have ensured our rise into an intelligent and wealthy species has been very well documented. All events, including wars or invasions, having been meticulously accounted for to ensure success to the winning side is celebrated; the underlying tone behind this is always power, wealth and strength of manhood and prowess. All aspects of maleness and its might and intelligence are condensed using the power of the

---

[1] The Sybils (The First Prophestess' of Mami Wata)

written word. Most of our fifth root race legacies has been divided into two brief eras. There is BC, Before Christ and AD, Anno Domino, Latin for 'in the year of our Lord'. I guess when you examine this, it seems the modern man indeed is commemorated by his religious beliefs, especially in the eyes of Christianity, Catholicism and Islam.

Christianity became fashionable between the years of 31BC and around 30AD when Christ died. It is a human-manmade religion derived from plunder. The Source of Roman Catholicism comes from Egypt. It was the Abrahamic religions that diminished Iyami and the protection they offered here on Earth. Surprisingly, the biblical scriptures do not make the basis for a human-made religious faith, as the scriptures superimposed the esoteric traditions. Contradictively, the Biblical scriptures are rooted in retold Kemetic accounts. Within this, Christians do not figure at all, and each scripture became rewritten after the ensuing invasions occurred along the desert trade routes.

The Knights Templars infamous crusades throughout the ancient world, based their ritualistic practices on the principles they discovered in Kemet and East Africa, these became the basis for the early Masons. The Freemason Organisation, then and now are based around the Feminine mysteries.

Regarding humanities more extended history, we could consider a much later timeline of around 4.3 million years of evolution starting with an entity that began walking upright to the now better-known *Homo erectus*, originating from approximately 1.8 million years ago.

There seems to be only a slight mythical sympathy towards humanities existence, its social status and incredible abilities celebrated beyond the history of Ancient Civilisations, this lack of knowledge has taught man to acquiesce in his ignorance. Yet it seems to be the least talked about in mainstream educational facilities. Though we acknowledge, Ancient Civilisations timelines from around 4,500 BC, Namely Ancient Mesopotamia, the Ancient Grecian Civilisation from 3,000 BC, and the Indus Empire around 2,500 BC,

Ancient China, Kemet and Nubian and Aegean Civilisations from 2,000 BC, Mesoamerica around 1,500 BC, Ancient Andean Civilisations and Ancient Steppe Empires from about 1,000 BC. Yet, so much is unknown about the more profound essence of the Feminine mysteries which underpinned these ancient societies.

Nevertheless, what do we know about an older Ancient world and its history? One now prone to mythic status. Perhaps I should ask, even though many scholars have researched and documented Ancient history, how much has become included and part of the history and geography curriculum taught in our schools?

The lack of accreditation to the matrilineal and Feminine mysteries, should be essential learning of who women were before the Patriarchal systems became the norm. Of course, there are references to Ancient religions; these usually include a somewhat debasing or subservient viewpoint, especially if it dares to usher in the premise of any female hierarchy let alone feminine driven worship. If we were to explore a brief and quick swipe through of our global history, it seems, much of any admission of a female based religion, is little known, beyond a degrading assumption that these females are famously better known as witches or sorceresses. Is it fair to assume we have forgotten how crucial women were and how revered they were in the Ancient world? After all, kings would not have become Kings without the influence of the Divine Mothers Priestesses. Her Priestesses were the renowned Counsels, and their oracles consulted before any significant pronouncement was made. Where can you learn about this information, and why has there been such denial and acknowledgement?

The patriarchy certainly conformed to type and accessed his inner nature, which ushered further what happened. Jealousy and an endemic desire for dominance expediated his need to become the sole owner of the feminine mysteries, which of course was also, fuelled by his greed.

It encouraged the masculine invaders and seekers to literally 'wipe out' all traces of a feminine religion. Replacing it with the now conventional human-made faiths, we are accustomed to; Hinduism, Judaism, Christianity, Catholicism and Islam, naming a few of the familiar leaders.

Matrilineal Religions and Sacred Feminine Mysteries

Clarification or knowledge delves into the hypothesis beyond compiled datelines. Though if we put an approximation of presence, we can offer a few facts. One, Ancient history records an early known civilisation having existed around 4,500 BC, these were the people known as the Sumerians from Ancient Mesopotamia.

Sumer[2] is the earliest known civilisation in the historical region of southern Mesopotamia, modern-day southern Iraq, during the Chalcolithic and Early Bronze ages, and arguably the first civilisation.

Period: Late Neolithic–Middle Bronze Age
Dates: c. 4,500–c. 1,900 BC
Geographical range: Near East–Middle East

The Sumerians are legendary and known as being an evolved race of humans, who among their other achievements and credits include developing Cuneiform, a system of writing, known as a wedge-shaped style of writing and they are written about in the biblical scriptures,

However, myths and stories exist, which predate even the evolved beings of Sumeria.

I want to include one we have all been captivated with, which is the story and lore of the rise and fall of Lemuria (MU) and Atlantis. Atlantis is for some people a mere conspiracy theory. In contrast, for others, it is a plausible example of an earlier prototype (or root race)

---

[2] *Sumer*

of humanity (a more previous experiment if you like) and its attempt to succeed or fail as the legend unravels.

To look deeper into what happened when Lemuria (MU) and Atlantis fell. The answer lies in the information we do know about these legends, Even to summarise how humanity lost its connection with both the natural world and the benign entities who worked alongside them, becomes a purgatorial repetitive occurrence in the tales of human existences. We also know, its demise happened when power and greed became far more critical than its spiritual evolution. Furthermore, its decline should be ascribed to the incoming mixed lineages from other star systems.

We could easily make comparisons today when we speculate about the fall of our modern civilisation swapping ecology for materialism and money, and greed and power instead of humility and wisdom. If we talk repetitive action, we are probably on version 5 or 6 of humanities folly or lack of learning from its previous experiments and its mistakes.

Lemuria (Mu) and Atlantis

ATLANTIS was a legendary island region in the far west which was sunk beneath the ocean by the gods by way of punishing the Atlanteans for their immorality, and willful disregard of justice and Universal laws. The story of the Golden Age of Lemuria (MU) and Atlantis unfolds here:

The Golden Age commenced within the third middle root race that stemmed from the Tree of life, The Lemurian and subsequent Atlantean kingdoms existed within an overlapping period. The Lemurians (also known as the water people) came first and were the Fathers of the Atlanteans. They were a race of third root beings, who were tall, had red skin and didn't hold any beliefs. It is an age deemed as 'a time when Gods walked the Earth, mixing freely with man'.

Over time, this middle third root race spread into becoming the Fourth root race, wherein these beings divided and blended with other creatures, creating mixed breeds of people.

The Bible Has Mentioned These Creatures Here

"The Bible account says that 'the sons of the true God began to notice that the daughters of men were beautiful'. (Genesis 6:2) Those 'sons of God' were spirit creatures who rebelled against God when they 'forsook their proper dwelling place' in heaven, materialised human bodies, and 'began taking as wives all whom they chose'.—Jude 6; Genesis 6:2.

The hybrids born from this unnatural union were no ordinary children. (Genesis 6:4) The Nephilim were giant bullies, tyrants who filled the Earth with violence. (Genesis 6:13) The Bible describes them as 'the mighty ones of old times, the men of fame'. (Genesis 6:4) They left behind a legacy of violence and fear.—Genesis 6:5; Numbers 13:33."

Who Are the Root Races?

There are seven root races or evolutionary cycles through which humanity evolves. Each root race divides into seven minor periods called sub-races, which again become subdivided into seven branches or what's known as family races. These sub-divisions are related to our now modern concept of races and ethnicities.

The first root race was (Polarian) This first race was 'Ethereal', that is, they were composed of etheric matter.

The second root race was (Hyperborean)
The third root race was (Lemurian)
The fourth root race (Atlantean)
The fifth root race (Aryan)
The sixth root race, as yet unestablished
The seventh root race, as yet unestablished

A timespan applied to a root race is considerable. For example, the Fifth root race, according to Theosophical records, covered the years 10,000 BCE to 3,000 BCE in right-brained megalithic cultures and 3,000 BCE to 2,400 CE in left-brained modern cultures. Do you notice how the fifth root race is Aryan? Rewind to World War II and Hitlers obsession with creating a world consisting of only a white, blond Aryan race of humans?

Ayran Understanding

In the encyclopedia 'Brittanica'. The translation of the word 'Ayran' means 'a people who speak an archaic Indo-European language'. They settled in Ancient Iran and Northern India. The German Nazi's, assumed this term to describe 'a white race of blonde, blue-eyed superior people'.

The ancient origins of the 'Ayran' race come from pre-historic Iran who migrated to India around 1500 BC. It is a word whose root is Sanskrit, linked to a Persian word 'Eran'. The social conditions were indeed comparable to the Sumerian culture and in areas, superior to the contemporary Sumerians and the Egyptians. Wherein, its religion surfaced around 5,500 BC; Agriculture came in around 4,000 BC, followed by Urban townships around 2,500 BC.

More Explanation of the Root and Sub-Root Races

These five root races stem from the Highest or Source, the 'I AM'.

The first ethereal race could self-create and didn't have vocalised speech.

The second race were beings with yellow or golden skin who could communicate using sound and a one-syllable speech.

The third race was the egg born, races of separate sexes of male and female, (Lemurian).

The fourth race were Atlanteans, born with a spark of a higher wisdom.

The fifth race is the race of modern humans we now are.

The sub-races were intermediary levels within the primary root races of existences and evolution. Better termed as having slight variations of the root race. Who would often have different racial backgrounds, and would exhibit small deviations to their abilities, while still falling into the category of the first root race.

Man Sees Himself as God!

During Atlantis, humans began to build temples that portrayed a phallic representation of themselves and their anatomy. Perhaps this was due to an over-inflated ego and an intense need for power or was it merely sensationalism of man's prowess in being able to replicate themselves via their seeding and sex, therefore by creating life in the females' wombs. This misconception provided the masculine with an over-inflated sense of grandeur and creative power, equal only to the Gods. Here we find the phallic representation of the Male Appendage, becoming the all-powerful giver of life. Thus in their minds, they were as powerful or even more so than the Creator. This example begins man's fascination concerning his endemic egotistical nature.

Perhaps this was the beginning of the influential patriarchal obsession with himself and the need to control everything, including the sacred mysteries?

Mystery Schools

Western esoteric traditions come from the Golden times of Africa and the Middle East, but having first spawned out of the ancient civilisations of Lemuria and Atlantis. After the fall of MU, Master Magicians, Alchemists and Priests having foreseen the fall coming, gathered up the mysteries and its secrets of Creation and concealed them in an attempt of maintaining its purity. They escaped the deluge. These people were mainly melanated (brown and black-skinned). They re-emerged in Atlantis bringing with them the pure esoteric teachings, containing pure magic from Lemuria. They built mystery schools and temples and became the Priests and teachers of Cosmic Creation and the pillars of the temples. They showed the Atlanteans the way. The Atlanteans were a fair-skinned race, located in a colder part of the world. The DNA of the Atlanteans was a mixture of Earth and Annunaki star bloodlines. They eventually began to gain mastery of some of the Lemurian pure magic and began to mix it with the Science of their star seeded DNA of the Annunaki, which did not contain emotional empathy.

It was the beginning of how sacred magic becomes a powerful ego-based entity and inevitably becomes corrupted. However, the story isn't all doom and gloom, as some pure-minded Atlanteans helped the original Priesthoods (comprised of mostly Lemurian and some of the purer Atlanteans), hide the secrets of the authentic mysteries. All of whom escaped the deluge, and eventually re-emerged and became the teachers and architects of later civilisations. These being the ancient civilisations found in Egypt, Babylon (Sumer), Persia, Kemet and Nubia, South America, India and Greece. These Priests established mystery schools that attracted some of the gifted healers of due wealth from the Hyperborean and Celtic Lands. Eventually, these gifted healers took the knowledge of the mysteries they had learned in the mystery schools back to their lands.

When they returned home, they used the knowledge, and it elevated and transformed the basic indigenous Priesthoods, namely the Druids of the Celtic lands and the Gauls, into a complete system of learning—raising Druidic orders from primitive knowledge to having a more evolved and sophisticated knowledge of the Cosmos. It did the same in the Nordic Lands, through the influence of the gifted Hyperborean healers who had attended the Mystery Schools.

Evolutionary Demise of Lemuria and Atlantis

Lemuria and Atlantis spread their civilisations throughout the lands. Mu would build their cities from rare metals and Lava. Creating images of themselves out of black stone and then worshipping them. By the time Mu fell, the Lemurians were in their sixth sub-root race of evolution. It was likely Mu's destruction occurred by fire or a volcanic eruption or even a meteor strike.

The Atlanteans diminished in the Great Flood, most didn't survive, though a few of the most Sacred Hierarchy did survive and headed to Egypt.

The term 'Atlanteans' was also applied by the Greeks to the Phoenician colonies along the Barbary Coast of North Africa—i.e. those living near the Atlas Mountains. Diodorus Siculus describes their Titan-mythology and wars with the Libyan Amazons. Plato may have the same nation in mind for he named the second Atlantean king Gadeiros after a famous Phoenician colony near the Straits of Gibraltar. Some say that Atlantis was the Minoan culture that were around 2,500 BC–1,600 BC, while other sources, state it existed about 9600 BC. Either way, myth or reality, there is always a moral at the end of any story.

Man's Evolutionary Cycles Always End

There is further understanding of man's descent from grace, whereby grace, in this case, symbolises his fall from a state of incorruptible purity. You see, man has now become corruptible. He has sold his soul for need, dominance, pleasure and gain. He has given up his residence in the Garden of Eden because simplicity and bliss weren't enough. Why? Perhaps we can find part of the answer behind the King Arthurian Legends.

In ancient times, storytellers or bards (part of the Druidic clans) would travel from village to town, telling the stories about what happened in the other Villages or the Capitols, in exchange for food and a bed for the night. They were the talking newspaper of the day, and it is how the myths and legends spread around the country. The Legend of King Arthur is one of them.

In the days of old, there was a clan of beings called 'The Bear Clan'. They initially came to Earth from the star system Arcturus. Arriving in the time of early Atlantis throughout the time of Albion, (Albion was the old pre-Celtic name for England). The Bear Clan came to establish codes of honour, better known as chivalry attributed to the Knights of the Round Table and to bring forth a religious science to the land of Old England.

By the way, the law of cause and effect works, to be able to form any new Era, there must always be the right circumstances, and events put into place.

The King of Albion was Uther Pendragon who was married to Igraine. He loved her very much, and she birthed one son, called Arthur Pendragon, though in truth she birthed two sons. Twin aspects, where one entity is of the other, I will explain later. Igraine was then killed. Before marrying Uther, she had initially been married to the Duke of Cornwall. Uther asked 'The Merlin' to transform him into the Duke of Cornwall, so he would be able to meet Igraine and sleep with her secretly, and this is how Arthur was conceived. Later on, the Duke of Cornwall was killed in battle, and Igraine was free to marry Uther.

Arthur was given to 'The Merlin' to raise as his son?, was this a possible payment for The Merlins earlier help? Quite likely, however, a more viable reason would be to allow Arthur to receive an education from the Druids, who at the time had many esoteric schools. When Igraine dies, Uther was beside himself, and in his grief, Uther Pendragon banishes all magic from Albion. The old religion was dead along with all use of magic. Druidry ceased to exist, due to the fear of persecution. It is here our human pineal gland, begins to calcify. Reading this legend helps us see beyond the story and to be able to investigate a more profound conclusion.

I use the term 'The Merlin', because contrary to how we perceive Merlin, perhaps as a single old man with a long white beard, who wears greyed robes, tied around the middle with a knotted sash. Merlin is, and of himself, not a singular person, he is a group, hence the term 'The Merlin'. He is part of an old Druidic sect that perform magic and use herbs and potions.

Eventually, Uther Pendragon dies, and Arthur returns to court to take his rightful place as King. Here is where the meaning behind the sword in the stone comes to light. On Uther's death, the old era end is marked ritualistically by his sword being thrust into a piece of marble. To prove he is the rightful heir, Arthur must retrieve the sword from the stone. Here is where we must understand the symbology mentioned here. The sword placed into marble signifies the old era has concluded. Whoever retrieves the sword from the stone successfully achieves two things, one is that he proves he is the rightful King and heir, and the other is the symbolical start of a new era. Arthur does retrieve it and becomes King Arthur of Albion.

The Two Aspects of Arthur

Arthur is now King and has two crucial aspects within him. First, he is the Old Kings son and second, he was brought up, with The Merlin in the ways of the Old Religion and its use of High Magic. Throughout his reign, Arthur faces many challenges and is conflicted often with options. He faces decisions in remaining loyal to his upbringing and his teachers, and he is also accountable for being weighed by the scales of Divine justice, to ensure balance. Cause and effect create our karmic load. Eventually, he meets Guinevere, and they get married. Now here is where the masculine further their history, as King Arthur accompanies his Knights on long Crusades and battles. He is leaving Guinevere at home to play home keeper. Famously, her role doesn't keep her amused, and she has an affair with Lancelot, one of King Arthurs, trusted Knights and friends.

Another female of importance is Morgan le Fey, a possible cousin or even a sister to King Arthur. When magic is banished, she becomes outraged. On further examination, I feel it isn't merely due to the demise of the Old religion, though perhaps it is her lack of being acknowledged as a woman and her role in the court. Is Morgan Le Fey an actual felon here, labelled as a villain and a purveyor of the dark arts? Or is she merely another representation of a significant female who is fighting to keep the old religion alive? It is precisely the same as Lilith, Adams first wife, who famously would not lie beneath him. She has been turned into a legendary villain also, replaced by the ever-obliging subservient Eve.

The moral symbolisation of this legend, reveals itself in the Fall from Purity and being at one with the Divine, through High Magic. A choice was made to hold onto dogma and to evolve the linear mind, in a belief of conquests and colonisation, making up for the emptiness created by the loss of the old ways and Pure Magic. The masculine could only satisfy himself in the subjugation of nations and sexual conquest, and the feminine could only satisfy herself in a desire to be noticed and yearned for due to her sexuality. The stage becomes set, and our fates are now etched in stone. The masculine holds the reigns of dominance, and the feminine has surrendered all her powers and sacred secrets.. The powerful feminine archetype, as in Morgan le Fey, retreats to the Underworld. She leaves centre stage because she will not surrender to the patriarchal doctrine now in place.

The Goddesses Must Rise!

It is the truth we seek or even an acknowledgement, and I feel we should bring it to the fore. Women have endured centuries of being degraded, belittled and ignored. There has been so much manipulation of their gender and their diminishing roles in society. Even today as I write this it is the year 2020, and there has been a small amount of transparency towards men, revealing how much sexual abuse and sexualisation of women's bodies has been endured and exploited, and this is still ongoing. However, there is one crucial aspect I would like to mention, 'it is not about feminism or even the rights of women, I mention here'. I believe women have trod a long winding path to prove themselves equal. Yet while demonstrating their validity and worth, much has become lost in a battle between men versus women. So much so, it is fair to say, and this will cause a lot of controversies. Women have separated themselves towards the edges of reason, in ensuring they do not need men in their lives, whether this is for partnership or procreation, as we watch the state of play in the term of relationships and social interaction and behaviours.

Here I should add a disclaimer, as I recognise there is still a lot of injustice in society purportrated by misogynistic views of women. The influences that contribute to such treatment comes, of course from old beliefs and antiquated thinking. The traditional explanation is rife as many of the older generations have brought up their young within such a stoic belief system. Based on this belief, we can say the main contributor to this comes in the lack of a more comprehensive understanding or knowledge of our truthful rights and extensive history. It is easy after all, to go along with a viewpoint when all our schools teach is a patriarchal set of ideas within society. Until now, humanity can base its assumption and action on a relatively short time frame, yet this will change. Knowledge is the power they say, and in this, there is a comfort when we realise change is always an option.

Knowledge about our extensive history has indeed become lost and ignored; diligently swept under an enormous carpet. Hidden from view, for fear it becomes the standard and causes a rebellion, which would rock nations.

The Divine Mothers, Iyami, demand for this forgotten history to become more widely known, they feel humanity has lost its essential self. Humanity has endured a 'soul loss' of epic proportion and needs to now right this wrong before it is too late, and Iyami rises once more to take matters into their own hands. The Earth can easily wipe us, humans, off the face of her body, and it will regenerate and start over again. We are expendable, our fortunes, iPhones and our power, cannot save us from her wrath. She could wipe us away in the blink of an eye. I feel by the way 'Iyami have influenced the writing of this book, is a chance, possibly a fortuitous break, sadly to an inevitable end. Perhaps, in regaining our lost history, both women and men, must now join together and bring the whole of humanity back from the brink.

Chapter 2
We Are Iyami; We Are Sacred!

To introduce them or to even dare to speak their name, comes with great respect and a little trepidation. Though there is a guiding permission given to me to write about them and the Muses, watch over my shoulder to help me pen these words. The reason for saying this is to help you the reader understand how little we know about the Divine Ancient Ancestral Mothers as their existence is shrouded in profound and sacred mystery—those who serve them by being in service here on Earth. See them as both benign and benevolent beings who do not usually manifest. However, they can take on the humanoid form when needed. Spreading into all races, from the very beginning of Creation to share, heal and offer wisdom to the world to restore balance and order, through the scales of divine justice. By even saying this, I shouldn't deter your thoughts from this aspect; we should not rest on our laurels, or become comfortable in thinking they are 'alternative' in a new age state of mind. These Ancient Mothers can and will turn on or punish their children with the help of The Divine Lords of Karma, in the blink of an eye, especially as there is so much disrespect and lost souls abound in humanity right now.

Who they are and where they came from belies all manner of non-ordinary thinking and spans unfathomable supposition of time and space itself. Furthermore, we describe the Mothers as the keepers of the Cosmos and the guardians of the inner Earth. They spawned humanity from the very beginning of time, procreating with the masculine seeds from the Fathers of Sirius and Pleiades.

To explain further and I want to make this statement, Iyami are the Mothers of Creation, older and more ancient than any human-made history myth or religion. Additionally, they predate all false aspiring patriarchal gods; they do not belong in the alternative, Pagan or new-age realm or genre either. Because before their existence, there wasn't anything else of substance let alone such a thing as religion. It is fair to say they were the first beings and ensuing bringers of a primary and pure doctrine. Who they are, is more sophisticated and complex and should not be approached using a rational mind, but rather by using the textures and maps found only in your soul stars, and only If the soul can relinquish itself away from its limited matrix. To be able to do this, you must have an uncanny understanding of the type of surrender necessary.

To know or dare I say to become introduced to the Divine Mothers involves submission beyond the matrix of ego and the mind. When one has undergone the necessary surrender of ego and let go of all old belief systems and lack of trust, the brain has a chance to 'get it'. Finally, when this happens, such an explosion of synchronicity can occur, and its magic and power has to be lived to be understood.

You may appreciate how the patriarchal matrix has created its illusion, one which has become etched within our karma for millennia and throughout many past lives. Fantasies that have stretched us beyond our innate capabilities and gifts, towards a more rigid religious belief system, built on the powers and constructs of the mind and its perspective. We have traded our abilities for a divisive interpretation of the 'Word of God', we have sacrificed our feminine powers in obedience to man's laws and edicts. We have forfeited our prowess in magic and seership out of fear of reprisal. And it is in this alone, we allowed ourselves to prostitute our sexuality in exchange and barter for man's favour and protection. Our Femininity has become compromised as a second class companion to a so-called 'elite' race of masculine usurpers.

To show the Divine Mothers and who they are in their primary energy form, would entail a leap of faith on the part of some. If I could paint a picture, I wouldn't be able to do justice to my interpretation or be able to capture an Incomprehensible energy force, and I feel, would only disrespect their magnitude.

How then do I describe our Divine Mothers who birthed humanity?

To explore a better definition of knowing 'The Divine Ancestral Mothers', would perhaps involve a foray into the vastness of the Universe and its mysterious inhabitants. I am one who does not go along with any idea that earth humans are the only living beings in the known and unknown existence of the Cosmos and its multiverses. I say it's an impossible hypothesis to contemplate. If the idea wasn't right and we were, then we would surely be extraordinarily unique and of course, vulnerable to our need for survival in the future.

Who we are and where we came from is both a secret and sacred mystery. If told, wouldn't be believed. Maybe by a small percentage of independent thinkers. Though currently only a relatively low rate of around 2% of human beings are presently awakened. To better term, the phrase awakened here is the meaning of being 'awakened'...

Most of us probably remember the famous story about the Buddha, in which he is asked, "Are you a god?"

Buddha replied that he is not a god.

"Well, then, are you an angel?"

"No, I am not an angel."

"Are you a guru or a holy man?"

"No, I'm not even that."

"Well, then, what are you?"

To this, Buddha replied, "I am awake."

The Oxford English dictionary defines the word 'awake' as 'to come out of the state of sleep'.

Furthermore, the spiritual sense of awakening refers to becoming consciously aware of reality, as opposed to the ordinary physical sense of shifting from nocturnal dream illusions to daytime experiences induced by perceptual shortcomings in consciousness. Just because most of humanity continues to fool itself into considering appearances as reality does not excuse us for our continuing self-deception. All such self-deception has a price.

To appreciate the maths surrounding the actual number of people across the globe who no longer view reality in an ordinary sense. Is to do the maths; there are 7.5 billion approx. Inhabitants in the world and even with such an ever-increasing and decreasing amount. It infers 150,000,000 million people have awakened spiritually and are open to suggestions about this esoteric possibility beyond self-deception and who may understand the impact of such knowledge of our Creation.

More importantly, there are ruling councils in the Universe who can and do make an impact on Earth. These include the Sirians, the Pleiadians and the Lyrans. This sentence will, of course, place some of you outside a familiar comfort zone. Evidence indeed exists from our 'First Nations peoples' who knew of these star beings and believed they impacted earth-life. For example, the Andean cosmovision of their evolution share these esoteric teachings about their ancient cultures, which says, the divine aspect of human form and consciousness came from the stars and that the Pleiadians & Orions provided the energetic blueprint for the human consciousness' or codes of light hidden in our DNA.

Iyami are the universal guardians of humanity. They arrived here on Earth, after travelling from the Planetary Systems of Vega, to Pleaides, to Sirius B and Venus, most came via Sirius. When they came here, they held court with Mother Earth (Pachamama) the Divine owner of the land we tread, the meeting was held within a place of magical trees indigenous to West Africa, these were the Sahel and

Mangrove forests, which still stand today. Where a deep reverence for the Mothers has hardly waned at all in these societies, it is here, Iyami arrived via their portals onto Earth. Today it is in these most sacred of groves, where ceremonies are occurring to help restore balance in the world. Reverence to the Mothers is eternal, as is the restoration of balance here on Earth.

Iyami have a core council, who are 'Super Creator Goddesses'. I will reiterate, they are not human, and neither is their DNA. Iyamis DNA contains Divine-God sequences.

On their way to Earth, the Mothers descended from the Highest God throughout the star systems. Along the way, they visited many of the 'Goddess Temples' located on the planets Sirius, Venus and Pleiades. Here they gathered star DNA. And it is while visiting these planets they often coupled with other Super Gods before making their way to Earth.

On their arrival on Earth, they carried with them a mission, which was to charge and aid Pachamama, they shape-shifted into pure Earth or Divine dust, to help with the Creation of her human children. Achieved by seeding Earth with their Divine-God Sequences, mixed with the soil from the Earth and water from the oceans, creating humanity as we know it. The age of the Divine Mothers is unfathomably older than humans by aeons.

When the Iyami first came here to Earth, they mixed themselves with all four elements of Earth, air, water and fire. As the Earth was covered mainly with water, it was here they rooted their energies first. Creating their first kin, a Divinity known in Africa as Olokun, who has been recognised ever since as the Keeper of the Sacred Mysteries and the Owner of the secrets of the deep oceans.

Some of Iyami agreed to take form after the fall of Lemuria and towards the end of Atlantis to help Father God and the Lords of Karma establish justice and order, this happened after 'the fall of Atlantis'. Manifesting in form, they lived among humans. Some married Deities who were created after they were, for example, the Orishas of African

Etymology, the Greek Gods, the Egyptian Gods and so on. Some of their children, in turn, married evolved humans and those born of the last coupling, usually became the Priestesses/Priests, Master Druids and Master Shamans of the Ancient world. All of this was done merely so traces of their DNA and the DNA of the Most Highest God sequences can assist the tribes and clans around the world, after it has activated and awakened within the cells of the body, of Iyamis children. It is fair to acknowledge how most of Iyamis children are now the wayshowers here on Earth, present throughout history and even today.

All of this occurred after the fall, as the sacred lineages saved from the fall of Lemuria and Atlantis spread into Africa, both in Egypt, (Ancient Kemet and Nubia) and then via the desert trade routes into the West of Africa. Those safeguarded included the races of the 'Yellow beings', the 'brown and the black skinned' and some of the remaining red race.

In the West of Africa, a further race, noted as the fifth race was produced from her holy DNA. Iyami remained and ruled over the first Divinity clans of Kings. And it was at this time that this race is now known as The Serpent/Dragon (Reptilian) beings, known as Mami Wata (A Pantheon of Water Gods) who returned to Earth and made peace with the fifth race and taught them how to evolve and survive.

The Divine Mothers in African etymology are recognised by the title Iyami. The name Iyami refers to their spiritual powers and translates to 'My Mothers': Their sacred principles and teachings became the origin of religion in the now more familiar worldview systems of IFA/Orisha and Vodun systems. These traditions are endemic to the Religion of Benin Republic, Western Nigeria, Togoland Ghana and parts of Mali. IFA/Orisha originated in The Old Yoruba kingdom of Nigeria and Vodun originated from the old Dahomey Kingdom, now the present-day Benin Republic. The timeline for these source teachings came from over 12,000 years ago. These two lands are indeed part of the same coin and have been established and anchored by The Mothers or Iyami. Today these teachings are still intact in these lands, as are the mysteries of the Iyami, their complete body and mounds have been seeded and rooted here. The Mothers made a covenant for this to be so. As it provided the Iyamis from the Stars of Sirius and Pleiades a landing and meeting place and they became rooted there within their sacred groves. Their branches spread outwards to Mali and Burkina Faso and the rest of the world. Today, the body of Iyami's teachings exist within only a few families, who guard it fiercely after the denigration of matrilineal women was taught by aspects of Islam, which is now pervasive there.

Even to study the teachings of the Iyami in Mali today is very difficult, as the few families who do, guard their secrets well and they remain cloaked in profound secrecy, Only passed down through solid ancestral lines only to be safe and to defend it against Islamic incursion. However, in Benin, the teachings of the Mothers is practised openly, and in tremendous Royal fashion around the original mounds and groves. Here it is part of the Vodun state religion. Indeed Benin is favoured as one of the most peaceful lands in the world. These mystery teachings of the Iyami or Original Mothers exist only within a deeply shrouded secret inner sanctum and mere outsiders or those who do not hold part of their original DNA, cannot enter. Recognition of the star beings and how their influence was revered and known here on Earth continues to be the background of many first nations.

Getting to Know Iyami Better

To repeat, the Iyami are super goddesses who live in their sphere within the twelfth Dimension, also known as shamanic heaven.

They have been here since the beginning of Creation. Sharing wisdom and healing through the activation of the scales of divine justice. (The scales of justice are how the deeds and actions of humans are weighed). They are the universal guardians of humanity.

41

As I mentioned, Iyami came from Father/Creator God, known as the highest throughout the star systems, and they are also present in the core of the Earth, known to many as Shamballa. From here, after the fall of Lemuria and Atlantis, they went into East/West Africa, where they were present for aeons before spreading throughout the rest of the world. Humanities routes of migration and habitation spread from 100,000 years ago in Africa, throughout Europe and Asia, around 80,000 years ago, to Australia about 60,000 years ago, into North America approximately 40,000 years ago then into the most recent of all South America, between 10,000 and 20,000 years ago.

Iyami are also accompanied by Angels and some other God beings who joined them later to help with the task of bringing order, balance and justice to compensate for humanities many imbalanced ways. The need for balance, etc., occurred after the fall of man whereby regaining karmic balance was essential, it was here, The Divine Lords of Karma first came on the scene. Aeons before Lemuria. Angels and some of the very early humans became God beings joined Iyami later to create balance and justice, due to the influx of many unbalanced star beings and races. It was also where we are first seeing the phrase 'duality' making an entrance. Coined from the arrival of unstable beings coming to earth, for example 'the Grey lineages,' especially more towards the end of Lemuria, hence the need for a Karmic Board was born.

Iyami are the Primordial Ancient Mothers who were charged to bring the seeds of Humanity to Earth so a version of a human prototype could form. These seeds were planted as crystals inside the Earth in West Africa.

There are three groups of Iyami, who number 144 in each group. Though to fully understand their true nature is complicated, because it is exceptionally multi-layered and multi-faceted. They filter through a Divine head known as the Great Mother Simha, and even though they are mostly known in the African IFA/Orisha traditions, their history and cosmology are much older.

Iyami governs with the laws of nature as well as spiritual laws and Codes of conduct. Iyami have an inherent relationship with nature. Mother Earth, Mother Nature. The Cosmic Mother is known as Iyanla.

To relay any confusion to the much-hyped use of a Divine Feminine, including The Magdalene or Isis, or Mother Mary, etc. We understand that these are later manifestations of Iyami, who had taken human form throughout history. It was not until after the fall of man, after the end of Atlantis. That Iyami and the Lords of Karma came back to Earth to ensure growth through karmic resolution and compassion, to offer eventual freedom for humanity. A purpose that is taking longer than anticipated. Hence the need to understand and work more with Iyami.

An Introduction to Mami Wata

The Ancient Egyptians, Hopi Peoples and The Mayan People all focussed importance on the 'belt of Orion', building temples and pyramids in direct alignment to Orion. The Egyptians, uniquely named Orion and Sirius as being a 'place where the Gods descended from'.

It was the Ancient Dogon tribes of West Africa who notably created art that famously, details a specific being who came from the stars and lived in the waters. Arguably are these the same or similar beings that are mentioned and existed as part of many of the Ancient cultures history and creation myths, from West Africa, the Nagas of the Early Dravidian people of India, South America (Peru & Mexico), the Aborigines of Australia, Ancient Mesopotamia and so on? All of whom, mention in their myths about these water-based Ancestral Beings – ancestors who taught the original people how to survive, evolve hunt and how to live. In many ways, these ancestral beings became known as Prophets in the Abrahamic faiths, and many of them may well have been Prophets of God for the Aboriginal peoples.

Another essential point to mention regarding the knowledge detailed within the Creation myths of the Dogon Tribes (West Africa), Mesopotamia (Iran), Egypt and the Minoans of Crete. They all mention a half-man, half-fish being who came from the planet Sirius B. The Dogon tribes themselves are believed to be of Egyptian descent and whose astronomical law goes back to around 3,200 BC. They tell of a race of people who came to Earth from the Sirius Star System; they called these beings 'the Nommos' Depicting them as amphibious beings which resembled what we know today, as Mermen or Mermaids. The Dogon today believe the Nommos landed here on an Ark, headed to Earth from the belt of Orion known as Sirius or Sothis or which is more commonly identified as the 'dog star' when asked where their ancestors obtained stories about half-man, half-fish people, they say it was from Ancient Egypt.

In ancient Egypt, there is a well-known acronym ANKH, which is an Egyptian hieroglyph symbol meaning the 'source of life'. When I say acronym, it was common for the Egyptians to talk in these, you often see capital letters that do not fully spell out the word in full. ANKH is a prime example. When ANKH becomes articulated fully, it is indeed a secret chant used to invoke Creation and rebirth.

AA NU KA HE

Could this be a reference to the infamous Annunaki, mentioned in Mesopotamia? The Sumerians worshipped the Anunnaki, who were the children of Earth and sky; An, the sky god, and Ki, the earth goddess, these beings introduced the concepts of money, finance, and debt to human societies.

The Dogon name for Sirus B is Po Tolo, Po – meaning Star, Tolo, meaning Seed of Creation. The word Nommo means a group or individual spirit.

These beings came out of the water during the daytime and taught humans morality, how to hunt and fish, how to manage their land etc. They would return to the water at night. Ancient African cultures began to worship them as Gods and Goddesses, honouring them as guardians of Divine knowledge and law. However, as much as they taught real practice, they would also punish the tribe's peoples for breaking the rules set for humanity. These punishments were various and often cataclysmic in the form of floods. Perhaps an essential point to ponder is this:

"Is it possible to infer that early ancient humanity was merely an experiment if we needed these beings to teach us how to live?"

The relationship between humans and 'Nommos' developed further as humans began to worship them. After all, the water beings offered and gave so much for the tribe's people to be able to sustain themselves.

Nommos Mythology in Ireland

There is also a similarity between the Nommos mythology to the mythology of Celtic Ireland. Regarding one of their earliest tribes of people who noted the Tuatha De Dannan and their figurehead Danu. Danu is one of the oldest deities in Celtic Mythology. She is the Mother of the Gods and the Tuatha de Dannan, who were the first tribe's people who lived in Ireland, she is also their Protectress. Much of her history remains unknown with most of her myths and stories eventually forgotten. The oldest record about the Goddess having been documented in the Irish Lebor Gabala, from 1,000 C.E.

The name means wisdom or teacher and Danu is the Earth Goddess of Fertility and abundance, agriculture and cultivation. They are also known in Wales as the Goddess Dan. However, historians believe she has a connection to the water. The story of the arrival of the Tuatha De Danann, states they landed on a mountain in ships from the sky, again, doesn't this sound familiar to our earlier creation myth? The Tuatha were a remarkably evolved group of people who became held in high regard. These people possessed terrific domestic, arts, crafts and magic skills and became revered as magicians and Gods.

There is further evidence of African roots being here in Ireland. By way of 'The Fomanians', a name which means 'dark of the sea'. The Fomorians were likely to be the Cushitic people known for being sea-faring people, likely hailing from the Phoenicians or Egyptians and the lineage of Ham. However the Celtic myth of 'the Selkie' ushers the inference of a creature which is a seal by day and a human by night. The[3]Bible directly refers to Egypt as the Land of Ham. The word Ham is believed to come from the word Khawm which means 'black, hot, and burnt' in Hebrew and chamam, also a Hebrew word for 'to be hot'. *Ham is the youngest of Noah's three sons along with Japheth and Shem. Ham himself has four sons, namely: Cush (Ethiopia), Mizraim (Egypt), Put (Libya), and lastly, Canaan (Canaanites are believed to be the first people in Israel). The Bible stated that Ham and his sons, and their soon-to-be descendants lived and became the forefathers of the African continent and the Middle East.*

Significantly, Danu was usurped and demonised as a witch as soon as the Christianity, swept into Ireland.

Returning to Mami Wata

In African mythology, the Nommos/Mami Wata pantheons were praised as Gods and Goddesses. Identified by the title of Mami Wata, a name which later included a pantheon of Water Gods. The words translate to Mami (Truth/Wisdom) and Wata (Woman). We see these ancient deities endorsed as a far-reaching Matriarchal structure, who ruled throughout the ancient world for thousands of years, firstly

---

[3] https://amazingbibletimeline.com/

having a vast dominion in Africa. Pictorially seen as the half-human or half-reptile characterised throughout Africa and the Ancient world.

Further[4], we discover from Ancient Mesopotamian myths that the first great water goddess in the story of the Creation-Flood was known as 'Mami', (Mami Aruru) as she became identified in ancient Babylonian prayers as being the Creator of human life.

Furthermore[5], Massey informs us that the word 'Wata, Watoa, Wat-Waat' which means 'woman', are all exact spellings in the ancient Sudanic languages spoken by the Baba, Peba and Keh-Doulan groups. In ancient Egypt, Uati was Isis', oldest appellation, and was the first Mami goddess worshipped by the Egyptians as 'the Holy Widow', 'the Genitrix', the 'Self-Creator'. Celebrated as 'the one who reigned alone in the beginning', or 'the one who brings forth the gods'. Or, 'she who was mateless' and 'the Virgin' (meaning 'unmarried') Mother. Thus, we have Isis originally worshipped as 'Mama Uati' in ancient Egypt, and as Mami (Uati/Aruru) in ancient Mesopotamia, where she is first addressed and immortalised in prose by the gods.

We now understand more about the story of the Goddess Isis, who was one of the Original Divine Mothers and how Isis became usurped and re-packaged by Christianity as the Christians began to pen their creation myth. Whereby Isis, became reformed and seen as the Virgin Mary, the Mother of Jesus. This story was severely plagiarised and reconfigured.

The Goddess Isis was the ancient Egyptian goddess of marriage, fertility, motherhood, magic, and medicine. Her legacy and legends flourished throughout Egypt and were endorsed in its literature. As do the many other names she is known. For example; the Phrygians called her Pessinintica; the Athenians called her Cecropian Artemis, the Cyprians, identified her as Paphian Aphrodite, the Cretians,

---

[4]Dalley 2000, p 51-16, Stone 1976, p. 7,219
[5] Massey 1994, p248. Massey 1992, p204 ,227

remembered her as Dictynna, the Eleusians called her the Mother of the Corn, other names include Juni, Bellona, and Hecate. Is she the Danu from Celtic Ireland too?

Returning to the Appropriated Story, We Return to the Egyptian Myths

Horus was the child of Isis and the disembodied Osiris. Whom, Isis searched high and low for when he had become torn into fourteen pieces by Set. When Isis found Osiris, she used a spell to restore Osiris to life for one night. After intercourse, she conceived Horus, she finally gave birth to Horus on a papyrus bed and hid him from Set. There are numerous representations of Isis with her son, Horus, all of which bear a marked parallel to following images of the Virgin Mary with baby Jesus. As does the story of Isis having to hide Horus from Set, this again can be compared to Jesus having become hidden away in a basket made of bullrushes and placed into the river, so King Herod would not find him and kill him.

The Mami Wata Religion spread far and wide throughout and beyond West Africa. From Benin whose people are known as 'The Fon', to the Ewe people of East Ketu. To Sudan in the North, to Egypt, throughout Ethiopia, Yemen, Saudi and India, onward through black Libya. It then spread outside of Africa to Greece (Crete, Ionia, Minoa and Mycenae), Mesopotamia and Italy and even further throughout Asia Minor (Turkey). The name Mami Wata name became changed to other names throughout the different continents. Some of these names include Isis, Mami Awussa, Ishtar, Artemis, Queen of Sheba. Demeter and Black Diana. All of whom became endorsed in their ancient cultural myths.

When people term these religions as being Pagan, this cannot be the case. The word Pagan would infer it was merely an alternative religion. The word Pagan means 'A person who is holding religious beliefs other than those of the leading world religions. The worship of Mami Wata was the **only** religion at the time. And this is the issue we should focus on here as being one of the main facts which reveals itself as a 'religion' for want of a better word which underpins most of the early world religions. Symbolically spread from Africa to Ireland possibly, due to its reference to 'serpents and snakes'. Therefore in itself makes It surprising, it isn't recognised as an essential source across the world or celebrated as such.

After all the hype we have grown up with year after year, in celebrating the birth of Jesus as a date to be exalted and honoured and while this may be the case as far as the patriarchal viewpoint is concerned. Placing this aside is now apparently a disreputable case of blatant hijacking something and making it your own to gain favour, power and dominion. One should wonder how much more truth and lies we humans have been diverted away from?

It is also equally important to create a reference back to the half-man, half reptile beings who were so revered in early Africa. Especially as throughout the chronicles of cultural history, there are often many references to 'Serpent Worshippers', where many ancient cultures throughout the globe identify with the snake as a deity or significant symbol.

Wherever in the world, your ancestors were born, be it Mexico or Peru, you will find references to divine beings such as Quetzalcoatl, Cihuacohuati and Amaru. The latter were early inhabitants of Peru and originated from and around Lake Titicaca before the Incas arrived. Or in India or Vietnam who name Naga or the Nagin people as their serpent deities, known as beautiful women associated with lakes, sea and the trees. The Serpent deities were all seen as the original sacred feminine energy, which was synonymous with fertility, abundance, magic and medicine. All of these ancient mysteries, albeit stellar or solar mysteries, all reference back to the Divine feminine. The woman is of herself the mystery and the Source of all secret societies. From pre-dynastic Kemet in the East of Africa to the Dogon tribes of Mali on the West of Africa, whether you hail from the Old Kingdoms, Middle or New Kingdoms, your legacy and etymology hail from the Divine Feminine mysteries. These were only changed, altered and stolen when the Muslim, Islam, Greek and Roman invasions which spread through those desert trade routes, came in and wanted these mysteries for themselves.

Serpents and snakes and even dragons are all mutual symbols in many early religions. You can easily find the sacredness of serpent symbolism in many cultures; Ancient Egypt, Ancient Semitic, Ancient Babylonian, Ancient Assyrian, Ancient Greece, Ancient Iberian, Ancient Aztecs, Ancient Peruvian, Ancient Hittite, Hopi and Ancient Norse.

To elaborate a more delicate point, one credited to St Patrick of Ireland, whose infamous legacy is in his prowess to eradicate all the serpents from Ireland. Many think Ireland was awash with the slither and slide of snakes abound in the countryside. And again we acknowledge the genocide, and its dark arm is heralding its violent nature of patriarchal invasion and stealth.

In conjunction with the attack on the Old Druid Priesthoods in the Celtic lands of Wales, Ireland, Scotland, France and the Isle of Man, this violence was spreading throughout all ancient cultures of the world. All Celtic nations became victims to Christianity and its fervent desire to wipe all traces of the Divine feminine mysteries, symbolised by the serpent from ever existing. Otherwise, it would threaten the 'new kid on the block', the male in his new role of absolute and utter power and domination.

To embody the purity of Iyami requires us to wade through all of the off-shoots and derivatives of these magical mystery teachings. Who they are then and now has for many cultures become hidden and forgotten. These Primordial Mothers of Creation and the Cosmos, hold unfathomable powers. However, today's recognition of these authoritative beings has become lost in our human necessity to contain and own Deity and in doing so, become equal to it. Humans have placed themselves on a pedestal of importance, the very idea to bend a knee to such Divine Feminine powers or by any way becoming accepting of such power beheld within the sacred feminine mysteries. Let alone admitting to the calculated usurping of the Ancient Feminine Divinity, would see the patriarchy lose its grip on female domination and therefore lose its wealth and status. Though in saying this, I want to end this chapter to nurture seeds planted a long time ago, which states unequivocally 'She Rises, She Rises, She Rises!'

Chapter 3

Source – Father God the Most-High

With so much of Ancient history forgotten and resigned to the chronicles and hidden vaults inside museums and other secret places. It is a difficult task to try and understand how humanity has lived and evolved since the very beginning. We know how the scientists and even the Bible, explains how we came to populate the Earth. Our evolution is, of course, well documented and taught. Inside the Bible, in the book of Genesis, it propagates the beginning as:

"In[6] the beginning, when God created the Universe, the Earth was formless and desolate. The raging ocean that covered everything was engulfed in total darkness, and the Spirit of God[b] was moving over the water.[3] Then God commanded, 'Let there be light'—and light appeared.[4] God was pleased with what he saw. Then he separated the light from the darkness,[5] and he named the light 'Day' and the darkness 'Night'. The evening passed and morning came—that was the first day."

In six days, he proclaims:

"Then God said, 'And now we will make human beings; they will be like us and resemble us. They will have power over the fish, the birds, and all animals, domestic and wild,[d] large and small'. So God created human beings, making them be like himself. He created them male and

---

[6] Bible Gateway The Creation

female,[28] blessed them, and said, 'Have many children, so that your descendants will live all over the Earth and bring it under their control. I am putting you in charge of the fish, the birds, and all the wild animals.[29] I have provided all kinds of grain and all kinds of fruit for you to eat;[30] but for all the wild animals and for all the birds I have provided grass and leafy plants for food'—and it was done.[31] God looked at everything he had made, and he was delighted. The evening passed and morning came—that was the sixth day."

Indeed many of the 'first nation peoples', all have their own stories of Creation. Here is an example.

Native[7] American Creation Story
Cherokee

In at least three Cherokee creation stories, the world begins as a large, unexplored body of water. The only beings in existence are the animals, and they all live in the sky. In two of these stories, the Earth is a grand island floating in the water. In another story, the land isn't yet formed until the Water Beetle volunteers to go and explore what is at the bottom of the vast body of water and comes back with mud, which then becomes the land.

Other Creation Myths

Now, even though we tell this story from the perspective of the Native Americans, they were not the only people who went underground. The holy people all around this planet went underground. For instance, the Aborigines in Australia and those who were later to become the Druids in England were all preserving their knowledge underground as well. The Druids were safeguarding the old Atlantean information, as were the Egyptians. But the native

---

[7] Sourced from Wikipedia

peoples of the Pacific area, including Asia, were protecting the Lemurian information. These indigenous peoples, even today, hold within themselves this sacred knowledge. Some of it is conscious, but most of it lies in the subconscious. The Ainu of Japan is one of the tribes that preserved some of the knowledge too. There was excellent cooperation among the peoples of Earth to ensure these sacred teachings are known.

Creation Roots

The stages of evolution and consolidation to evolve into the fifth root species we are now, comes from the joining of Spirit and Matter, from Spirit, Soul, to the Physical body into a Cosmic and primary human form. The Angel Gods of the Four directions and other Chief Groups of Architects and builders come together from the primary root on the Tree of Life, The Divine Vehicle of God (Father Spirit) and the Divine Mothers (Mother Spirit), birthed the mind-born sons of the seven planets: Mercury, Pluto, Saturn, Venus, Uranus, Mars and Earth.

Hence we evolve to creating physical life here on Earth as well as on other planets. All Creation begins with a mineral encased in stone. Eventually, the magma seeps out and becomes lichen or vegetable matter, creating a germ or animal matter until it finally ends up in the physical form. Each of these stages is fuelled, as further changes occur with the help of the elements of the natural world; Fire and Air, Water, Earth and Aether. From our Father, the Sun and Mother Moon, the element of wind carries it down to Earth and the transmutational aspect of fire changes all of it into physical matter.

A man begins in non-physical ethereal form and manifests into a physical form covered in flesh. We start with self-procreation and end up with being the egg-born species we recognise today as human beings. However, during these 300,000 years or so, the human has evolved throughout several stages of different expressions of itself.

It was during the Primordial Adam and Eve stages. Aided along the way by the Angel Gods, The Divine Mothers The Elohim and Star Beings, and even some negative shadows fell into the mix, monsters and Dragons animal instinctual humans, have all been part of the makeup and DNA of the earlier root and subraces until the Divine Mothers implanted their DNA into the sacred gems mixed with Earth in West Africa.

Fact or Fiction

It is possible to say that the rise and fall of the Lemurian civilisation are believed by some people to be correct, although you may not agree with this? Especially as there are not any proven scientific documented facts to prove or disprove the existence of such a place. Many have gone on a quest to find this mythological continent. Throughout woman and man's earth walk, lost civilisations have been known to rise and fall – or just appear and disappear without explanation. As with Atlantis, one can only speculate as to what possibly happened, based on some archaeological evidence. Views or any of these facts come from legends and theories pieced together by researchers, and even by metaphysical channelings.

The fate of Lemuria, also known as Pacifica or Mu, is what Edward Cayce called Zu or Oz and is not unlike that proposed for Atlantis. It is much like the destiny of humanity foreseen in our timeline by prophets of old and modern-day clairvoyants. The legends are the same, a thriving, advanced culture that suddenly manifested out of nowhere. Their origins and downfall are linked to destruction when their continent sank beneath the 'sea' due to natural cataclysm and social imbalance.

Edward[8] Cayce

The period 18 March 1877–3 January 1945 was an American Christian mystic who answered questions on subjects as varied as healing, reincarnation, wars, Atlantis, and future events while in a trance. A biographer gave him the nickname, 'The Sleeping Prophet'. A non-profit organisation, the Association for Research and Enlightenment, was founded to facilitate the study of Cayce's work.

Some consider him the real founder and a principal source of the most particular beliefs of the New Age Movement.

Cayce became a celebrity towards the end of his life, and he believed the publicity given to his prophecies overshadowed the most important parts of his work, such as healing the sick and studying religion. Many challenge Cayce's alleged psychic abilities and traditional Christians also question his unorthodox answers on religious matters such as reincarnation, and the Akashic records.

Even though there is limited evidence to support, those who believe that Lemuria (MU) or Atlantis suddenly appeared as a nation with a full-blown culture, an illustration of this spawns many interesting theories, including visits from extraterrestrials who introduced a new species of genetically engineered humans to replace their slow-witted ancestors. However, there is a relationship and links to other creation theories some of which regale stories of our Source entrance here on Earth, being a result of a prototype designed by Gods or even an Alien species. However, these Alien species are in actuality, an evolutionary path concerning the original architects of matter. For us now in our human construct of mind-matrix, it is possible to see beyond humanity and to accept how we were once conjoined with Angels and Gods.

In the main, a lot of this information written is a metaphor, having originated in the research of other theorists regarding the philosophy of human creation theory; the common factor includes an

---

[8] Sourced from Wikipedia

overwhelming ideology of an organising principle, capable of linking the patterns of Creation and the fundamental elements to sacred geometry. These factors infer more significant organisation from a highly refined being who advances out of a spiralling consciousness. Can transform and create form from its higher harmonic frequency of thought to a much lower rate to create structure.

Again a fact remains, and this is one for discussion. There was undoubtedly an original Adam and Eve prototype, who was the geneticist of this prototype, would surely know the answer of humanities source. My research to discover the Source took me on many a windy road; however, there is something in the idea of our Source coming from the stars. After all, even the Bible infers something similar along these lines.

Yet the basis of all religions, though these are human-made, infer a Divine Source or a Creator God who is the figurehead of all cosmology and belief. If we deny this, then we deny our very existence and presence here on Earth and our place in the Greater Universe. Can we then still view this Divine Source as an aged older man with a long beard that flows down to his feet? No, of course not, because it only makes sense, to make the point a Creator of such magnitude, one who can create life and planets and space itself. Is in himself a tremendous energy source, which in itself is without physical humanoid form. Behind the Source of our life, breath and being is a Divine Intelligent Consciousness. One who moulds and creates us and all other living things into the creatures we are today. For whatever reason or need, we have been created for, is the mystery of all life. Our purpose is driven by an invisible intelligent soul, one who urges, provides and gifts us lifetimes of experiences.

Who Else Is Present on Earth?

There is a lot of open discussion regarding a 'Reptilian' influence here on Earth. Conspiracists detail its presence in the higher realms of human existence: Governments, Royal Houses, Financial Institutions, Conglomerates, to name a few. They are known to some as the Annunaki for those who have never heard about them, and other names include the Nefilim, Reptiles, or Greys to mention a few. Should we enter into the realms of such a complicated and contentious topic? Yes, of course, we should. However, we must examine the Source to discover what is the Reptilian reference referred to here.

The Anunnaki (also transcribed as Anunaki, Anunna, Ananaki, and other variations) are a group of deities that appear in the mythological traditions of the ancient Sumerians, Akkadians, Assyrians, and Babylonians. Descriptions of how many Anunnaki there were and what role they fulfilled are inconsistent and often contradictory. In the earliest Sumerian writings about them, which come from the Post-Akkadian period, the Anunnaki are the most powerful deities in the pantheon, descendants of An, the God of the heavens, and their primary function is to decree the fates of humanity.

Researchers on this subject have found a similarity to the Annunaki to another reference, discovered in both the Book of Enoch and in the Bible. The similarities are between the Nephilim and a possibility to them being none other than the Annunaki.

The [9]Nephilim, the product of the sons of god mingling with the daughters of Adam, the great Biblical giants, 'the fallen ones', the Rephaim, 'the dead ones'—these descriptions are all applied to one group of characters found within the Hebrew Bible. Who are the Nephilim? From where do the 'heroes of old, the men of renown' come?

---

[9] Bible History Daily

Genesis 6:1–4 tells the readers that the Nephilim, which means 'fallen ones' when translated into English, was the product of copulation between the divine beings (lit. sons of God) and human women (lit. daughters of Adam). The Nephilim are known as great warriors and Biblical giants (see Ezekiel 32:27 and Numbers 13:33)

I feel the need to mention this, and it comes purely from a necessity to understand and possibly accept an idea coming from such a well-known and publicised book, in this case, the Bible and how I the author can make such an assumption of Alien interference in our DNA?

It is vital to understand 'Mitochondrial DNA'. I offer a hypothesis to provide evidence for Alien interference in our genetics.

Mitochondria are structures found within cells that convert the energy from food into a usable form of energy our cells can use. Although most of our DNA is contained within the chromosomes within the nucleus, mitochondria do have a small amount of personal DNA. This genetic material is known as mitochondrial DNA In humans. The Mitochondria DNA is passed down from mothers to their sons or daughters. However, the curiosity here is to explain, we all come from a common ancestor. The research discovered how we could all trace our ancestry back to one woman known as Mitochondrial Eve, who is said to have lived in Africa during the Pleistocene period, which is between 100,000 and 200,000 years ago. Described as being our most common ancestor of all humans on Earth today, concerning the matrilineal descendant line. To understand this timeline better, 200,000 years ago was around the time of the second Glacial period called the Wolstonian Stage, which was 50,000 years after the first *Homo sapiens* existed and recorded. One hundred thousand years ago was when the early *Homo sapiens* arrived in the Middle East.

Allow me to return to the inference of being a genetic prototype.

There has been a lot mentioned in the annals of star seed research of our connection with several prominent planets and star systems. Those who come up time after time, include Sirius B (mentioned first by the Dogons of West Africa). What this tribe knew was that Sirius B is a triple star system, a long time before modern Science even found out about the existence of Sirius B. their mythology regarding their Creation includes how the 'instructor' Gods descended from Sirius and brought knowledge and wisdom to the Dogon tribes. The Dogon were not the only ones to mention these planets. The Ancient Egyptians also revered Sirius along with Orion as necessary, as they too believed their Gods came from Orion (Osiris) and Sirius (Isis). The planet Sirius is known as a dimensional doorway to other realms, namely the Planet Vega, known for its darker-skinned beings.

The seven-star system of the Planet Pleiades is also very well documented in the oral history of Peru. Where they believe in the cosmovision and interaction with the Upper Worlds, even in Andean terminology they view the governing worlds and dimensions as the Hanaq Pacha, the Upper World, the Kay Pacha which is the Middle world, this world and the Uku Pacha which is the Underworld. The three pachas represented three separate planes of existence, interconnected and bridged by both physical and spiritual/ mythological elements. Together, the three realms formed Inca religion, the concept of the Inca cosmos and the day-to-day Worldview of both the Inca nobility and the common man.

The Native American tribes, which include, the early tribes of the Dakota speak of Tiyami being the home of their ancestors. The Hopi called the Pleiades the 'Chuhukon' meaning those who stick together. The Navajo mentions the Pleiades as the 'Sparkling Suns' and as being the home of the Black God, and the Iroquois tribespeople, pray to the Pleiades for their happiness.

Something important to note is how the Pleiades is also mentioned in both the Bible and Hebrew scripts.

If we head over to the first continent of Africa and in particular South Africa, you will find they worship the Pleaides as the stars of rain, and there is an Aboriginal tribe called the Pitjantjatjara who refer to them as the wives of Orion.

However, there is a crucial aspect to discuss with the planetary system of the Pleaides. This constellation contains seven stars, and it is the place of birth for many Gods and Goddesses. The seven plants are Maia, the eldest of the planets, Electra, Taygete, Alcyone, Celaeno, Sterope and Merope which is the youngest and has connections to Orion. These Ancient civilisations would look up to the heavens and the Universe as guides for their daily lives. The alignments of the planets created a map upon which civilisations planned their seasons, for planting and harvesting over the changing year. They viewed God/esses as being both benevolent and severe, or good or bad. Their myths and stories would reflect their experiences of these star systems and who came from which star system and how they influenced humanity here on Earth.

To continue to proffer a hypothesis around how humanity became form. Perhaps we should continue to look to the cosmovision, shared by ancient civilisations. Whereby Sirus became one of our parents as did the Pleaides and Orion. To further explain the importance of ancient knowledge, let's journey to the Hopi Tribes of the Arizona desert. Again, some of the knowledge gained here comes from both the rock paintings found in American Southwest and their mythology. The story of the Hopi begins after their people faced some very severe cataclysmic weather systems, ice ages, floods and extreme tilts. They tell the story of how beings came from inside the Earth and saved their people. These beings brought the tribespeople down through underground passages to safety and fed them. The Hopi had a name for these creatures; they called them Anu and Anu-Nanki, which translates to Ant friends. There is also a similarity in how the Sumerians from Ancient Babylon named their sky God Anu. The Sumerians connect with the Anunnaki, those beings who once came to Earth from the heavens. A further association exists between the Celtic Mother Goddess, namely Anu or Danu.

The 'Ant' people are associated with Orion, and the Hopi depicted them in their rock paintings as entities with long gangling bodies, large eyes and bulging heads. Other comparisons to the 'Ant' people originate in the legends of the Maya, who tell of Ant-like entities who built their stone cities and had magical powers which they used to move massive boulders into place. A question now remains to be asked and proven, were the 'Ant' people a progeny to the earlier beings namely the Nephilim, especially if you consider the meaning of the word, Nemalim which means 'Ant'?

In comparison and to answer this question in an informed manner requires more investigation. We should understand more of the early religion instigated by the first Mothers to reside here on Earth and how their lineages became the backbone of these early civilisations and what happened to them.

The way of The Divine Mothers and how the religion known as Mami Wata, swept throughout the Ancient world. Would come off the back of a deep imbuing of connection, between the advanced beings and how they created a highly advanced civilisation here on Earth. Their teachings and insights would have sparked off such immense respect to the sacred dimensions and how these would integrate here. There is a story about the Seven Sisters of the Pleiades, which bears further explanation of how the Mami Wata religions became as powerful as they did.

The story was not just the male gods of Mount Olympus who were enamoured with the beauty of the Pleiades or the gigantic hunter Orion who also hungered after the attendants of Artemis. Orion felt confident in the chase of the seven sisters as their father was in no position to protect them; Atlas held the weight of the heavens on his shoulders. Artemis was not happy about the ravaging of her attendants by her family members, and certainly did not wish Orion to do likewise. So, Artemis sought the assistance of Zeus, and the supreme God would, therefore, change the seven Pleiades into doves. Orion though was a great hunter and managed to track the seven sisters down, so Zeus instead transformed them into seven stars. Even then, Orion, as the constellation Orion, still follows the Pleiades across the night's sky. Interestingly the mention of doves will come into the story later. For the Mami Wata religion, the first religion to become so influential across the globe, from Egypt to Mesopotamia, to Asia Minor to Greece and other parts of Europe. There would be many places of worship in the form of temples that arose in these areas. Within these temples would house the powerful Priests/esses and their attendants, Kings and nobility and Generals would seek the counsel of these gifted people. It was indeed the powerful Priestesses also known by other names, such as, 'The Sibyls' or 'The Pythia' or 'The Doves'.

The summary of the Source of all must be first clarified as in understanding a point of view. If we know there is positivity; therefore, there has to be an opposite, such as negativity. If there is light, then also there is dark. If there is right, then there must be wrong. It is the law of duality. The Source or Creator God had to have created both. The Universe and all life cannot exist without its opposite. If humans were created to live, then why wouldn't there be any other beings existing alongside us. It wouldn't make sense to deny this. Some entities exist to bring harmony and balance, and then there will be those who live to bring forth chaos and imbalance. There is a constant battle going on between Earths seedings, whereby individual entities seek to interfere with how life progresses here on Earth. For example, if the Source Creator of all life, has created us for an experiment, to see if humanity can live within the purity of oneness. We need to understand the possibility of those who do their best to instil fear into life, and its sole aim is to thwart the bigger plan. If the idea is to bring a new dawn of balance here on Earth, then you can bet your bottom dollar there will be an agenda behind the plan to delay the coming of the Golden Age.

I will explain this further in the book, as regards, how an imbalance of patterning has been placed over the original purity and existence of oneness, merely to achieve an undeniable end to all that is good and wholesome in this world.

Chapter 4
The Divine Matriarchal Truth, Law and Provenance

Having introduced Iyami, Our Divine Mothers, we can better understand a greater possibility, for some it fits congruently as truth, and maybe for others, it still involves an open mind in accepting our origin as coming from the stars. It is easy to appreciate how, the early civilisations, revered earler beings, including Mami Wata or the Nommos who came from out of the water to teach and provide moral conduct and survival. In return, I can see how early humans would view them, like primordial parents, and would acknowledge them as great gods/esses, therefore worshipping and honouring them. Yet now let us delve into exploring how this scenario would lead to an introduction for the first religion on earth.

After all, what does the term 'Religion' mean?

"The belief in and worship of a superhuman controlling power, especially a personal God or gods."

The pratice of worshipping a being who helped, feed and guide you would indeed become an act of reciprocity. Showing gratitude to the entities and perhaps making offerings as a way of appeasement, would be a way to ensure human survival. Having taught the tribe, how to grow crops or build shelters, make medicines, find water to drink, and how to behave as a society. Would be reason enough to honour the teachings received from the Nommos or similar. Not only did they teach survival, but they would also be shown how to navigate the stars and to read the universal maps to know when to plant and when to harvest. These revered beings would have shared knowledge of their origination in the heavens. It is also fair to assume the Nommos would have shared so much more with the tribe too.

Our evolutionary path stems from over 700,000 years ago. When *Homo erectus* evolved in Africa into a new human species, *Homo heidelbergensis*, who had a much larger brain which they used to create well-manufactured stone tools. It was this species that then moved outside of Africa and migrated to Europe, including Germany and England. They comprised of a much more robust build and had excellent hunting tools, seemingly well suited to dealing with the climate variations in Europe. It was the *heidelbergensis* who evolved into the Neanderthals approximately 250,000 to 300,000 years ago during the Wolstonian Stage, mentioned earlier.

It takes many different elements to come together before a human community develops to the level of sophistication, commonly referred to as civilisation. The first is the existence of settlements classified as townships or cities. First and most importantly you would need the ability to produce food and for this to be effective enough production for a large section of the community to be involved in more functional activities. Such as the construction of buildings and temples to worship in or even the creation of works of art. Vitally important would be to ensure the settlement had protection, it would be necessary to introduce a practice of skilled combat, and above all the management of a centralised bureaucracy capable of running the inner workings of this. Civilisation requires at least a basic civil service.

The more society evolved and became a civilisation, the easier it was for humans to spread further and further afield. In about 3,200 BC the two earliest cultures developed in the region where southwest Asia joins northeast Africa. Indeed it was the great rivers, which became a crucial part of the story. The Sumerians settled in what is now southern Iraq, between the mouths of the rivers, Euphrates and the Tigris. And Egypt develops in the long narrow strip along the Nile valley. These rivers not only provided the water to irrigate the crops in the fields but became the easiest way to transport goods and to voyage to other areas, especially the other early civilisations of India and China.

It was around 3,200 BC that the Dogon Tribe of West Africa (Mali), began to speak of the Nommos the half serpent, half merman entity an advanced species which is associated with the Sumerians and the other Mesopotamian cultures. The Dogon tribe are a heterogeneous ethnic group descended from a mixing of the ancient Egyptians of North Africa with various other sub-Saharan tribal populations. What ensues from these encounters with the Nommos is a matrilineal culture or religion known as 'Mami Wata', bearers of the Divine truth and wisdom. Mami Wata became synonymous and first lived in the depths of the sea, and some still do. However, the remainder took to the skies and into the ethers or higher octaves of the planet Sirius.

Mami Wata initially described as 'The African Mermaid', is a collective, a Pantheon of water spirits, worshipped initially throughout Africa. These spirits known by local names are indigenous to Africa and then throughout the first ancient nations. Her role then and even now, is to offer healing, protection and provision for her devotees. Her primary teachings included maintaining social order, by enforcing the divine laws on humanity and therefore ensuring spiritual growth and a harmonious balance ensued. A natural order whereby man could co-exist alongside Divinity and other more advanced beings would benefit all in a holistic sense of a well-balanced society. The ethos of Mami Wata is as a free spirit, who lives apart from other Orisha, Gods and Goddesses, yet her domain belies in the deep oceans of Earth. Her kingdom belongs to the unchartered depths, where no man could survive. Here then her safety is assured within the sacred waters.

Temple Cultures Begin

Temples began to be formed and linked to this African Divinity and were the places to experience the first creation of an ecclesiastical authority here on Earth. The Mami Wata, Pantheon are directly related to Iyami. The Divine Spiral below shows the chain of hierarchy. With Iyami in the centre as emissaries of the Divine Father God, to Mami Wata who returned to Earth to help humans set up civilised societies. To the bridge between human and deity the Sibyl Priestesses.

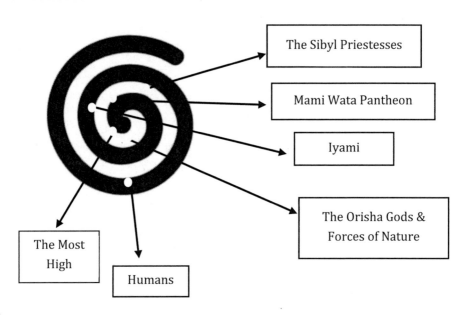

The Divine Spiral of Hierarchy

The temples were created in such a way to house the rituals and vessels, of communication and the ability to converse and receive direct guidance from The Mami Wata Pantheon, The Divine Mothers Iyami and The Orisha Gods/GoddessesThe bridge or intermediary was known as 'The Serpent Priestesses' or 'Sibyls'. These Divinely blessed human women created the temples and were consulted by the Rulers of the lands. The Sibyls had great powers; they were the initiated trusted vessels, between the seen and unseen.

Introducing the Sibyl Serpent Priestesses

The term Sibyl is an ancient term used for identifying a prophetess or Oracle and healer, and there were many throughout the Ancient World. They were the descendants of the first Neolithic clans, hailing from the African warrior-queens. They were sent from the Queen Mothers (Iyami) to establish the new land after the Great Flood. Here we, refer to how change occurred when a New root race was to begin. The Sibyls were high Priestesses. It was initially two black doves who flew from the ships towards Thebes (Greece) and Egypt after the demise of Atlantis. Their mission was to stabilise the Patriarchal aggression which threatened to unbalance and destabilise the natural and social Matriarchal orders on Earth.

The first Sibyl temple was built in Libya and the second in Delphi. The Oracle of Delphi is probably the most famous oracle we know. Her prophecies shaped political and sacred life within the forms of modern civilisation and helped define the course of history, though so much of this has been eroded in preference for myth and legend. Yet in Delphi at its height, no significant decision was made without first consulting the Sibyl at Delphi.

The Sibyls have been linked with caves or springs, both of which are symbolic junctions between the underworld and the earth, they could be older women or young maidens. These powerful priestesses continued to be consulted for over a thousand years. The Sibyl would use a method of going into a deep trance state, fuelled by the fumes of a potent formula. The work was always carried out inside the inner sanctum of a temple, whether this was a stone-built structure, a wooded grove or a cave. It was a pure female succession tradition, wherein the new Oracle would succeed her predecessor on her death, selected from amongst the inner sanctum of priestesses from within the temple. The temple maidens and priestesses were groomed exclusively within the temple. They were required to have had a sober and moral life, though it was possible to marry, this would, however, cease as would all other family connections, upon assuming their role as Sibyl. Each Sibyl was initiated into the higher mysteries before being reborn as Sibyls who were also known as Pythias.

The Importance of the Sacred Python

Mami Wata is generally depicted as being adorned with snakes. And the snakes are pythons which are sacred in West African belief. The python is considered a totem. And it is believed that the python is the manifestation of a Spirit being or deity. Each temple housed a sacred python. Therefore the temples pythons were essential religious symbols and highly respected. According to theology, a rainbow serpent is a vital deity that serves as an intermediary between the living and the spirits. Hence, the name often associated with the Sibyls is a Serpent Priestess. You will understand more about the significance later, which tells of how the Patriarchy, is hell-bent on slaughtering the sacred pythons across the globe.

Some of the Sibls of Note

The Cumaean Sibyl was the priestess presiding over the Apollonian oracle at Cumae, a Greek colony located near Naples, Italy.

The Erythraean Sibyl was the prophetess presiding over the Apollonian oracle at Erythrae, a town in Ionia.

The Persian Sibyl, also known as the Babylonian, Hebrew or Egyptian Sibyl.

The Samian Sibyl was the priestess presiding over the Apollonian oracle near Hera's temple on the Isle of Samos, a Greek colony.

Others include The Hellespontine, The Phrygian and The Tiburtine Sibyl.

There is more information in the next chapter, detailing the gifts of these Sibyls.

The Significance of the African Waters

When you fast forward to the slave trade, which swept through Africa, and how it affected those taken into bondage. We can appreciate the significance of being carried away over the sacred waters, which were so revered as the home of the first religion in Africa.

These are the waters, which later beheld the tears and sorrows of a diminished nation, turned into slaves who lost hope in ever returning to their beloved homeland again. Men, women and children in their thousands were torn from the arms and shrines belonging to their dear and honoured ancestors, in, a despicable and brutal Atlantic slave trade which was endemic between the seventh and nineteenth centuries.

Mami Wata, known by many other names and titles across the Ancient World and into the modern-day. Her names are different, yet etymology the same, from the continent of Africa to Mesopotamia (Iran), to Greece, to Turkey and throughout Europe. Now in the temples and shrines of misplaced Africans worldwide, she is worshipped as Mami Wata, Olokun, Yemoja, Simbi, La Baleine, La Sirene, Watramama, River Maids and Mamand'Eau. These names were revered and requested to maintain survival and to offer protection and to strengthen the spirits of the Slaves, as they endured the misery of captivity and other unspeakable experiences. Deep within the Diaspora of African people whose descendants made their home, in the countries of their slave masters. Mami has become part of a profoundly religious pantheon of Vodun and Yeveh worship. One with offshoots spreading throughout the Latin countries and her islands, call it what you will. Yet, its deeply shrouded mysteries, magic and divination and spells are a common belief of these societies. Widely accessible and genuinely feared by those who need the help and potions, to those who favour a modern patriarchal religion.

From the unchartered secrets held in the oceans, we now head to the heavens and the Queen Mothers who hold court here. These are the Divine Ancestral Mothers who came from the stars and birthed humanity. As the 'Queen of Heavens' and known by other names. The fantastic similarity and designation of these ancient goddesses are linked to a representation of provision. These being, the Queen, Fertility or Primordial Mother, the figurehead of agriculture or grain. All of which are basics supplements of civilisations needs.

A further essential part of the story and one of greater importance is to meet our Primal Mothers. The ones who made the first journey here and who came with a mission, directly given by Divine power. It is she we will know as Nana Bukken or Buruku (IFA Worldview), she originated from the etheric realms, Nana is a formidable member of the Greater Iyami sanctum. She used her unfathomable skills to work with the elements of air, fire, water, and earth to create a bridge between the Earth and the sky. Then by using her organising principles and expansive breadth of creation to carry the vibratory notes, necessary to develop the new dawn. Using vast amounts of energy and will she materialised a physical reality, by working with the alliances of the planets of Sirius, Pleiades, and Lyra. Then as head of her tribe, she sent emissaries, her daughters to earth to procreate and create a life here. It was she who directed the original Queen Mothers here to protect the integrity of humans. Nana Bukken is our primary Divine mother of both the universe and earth. If you look hard enough, you will find her near the rivers and the oceans. She is one of the Iyami, who can reverse time, look for her in the sacred groves.

A Prayer to Connect with the Primordial Mothers

By the law of love and the law of grace.
Iyami, my mothers.
With veneration, I call the mysterious Divine Mothers.
Oh, elemental spirits of abundance and sacred spirit of the Iyami,
Mothers and forces of definition, power, creation and the cosmos.
I honour you, the sacred society of elders.
I beseech you; please bring me and the ones I love, good health and
shields of protection.
I implore you; please dispel all negativity and sorcery away from me
and the ones I love.
I ask you to protect our home, land and all animals who have chosen
to be with us in this lifetime.
I ask you to protect all manner of transport used by me and the ones
I love.
By the law of love and the law of grace.
I offer this gift in your name and with sincere gratitude,

Leave out a small offering of water and honey mixed together.

Chapter 5

A Patriarchal Totalitarian Era

"We live in a world we know is no more than an act of faith."
Ross Heaven Shaman and Author

The masculine a gender who is comfortable in his capability to attain and seek out greatness. He in his role holds the gift of seed, a hidden key which helps to procreate life on our planet. Man can surely boast about his excellent adventures and achievements, especially in continuing the job of the 'Nommos' to ensure the 1st Neolithic humanity evolved and assured its survival. Man's strength is our protective shield, his bravery for quest and discovery is the stuff our nations have built themselves on. He is the ultimate warrior, a defender of kingdoms, and he is the edge of reason when all else fails.

After celebrating the masculine and his apparent gifts, we should ask why there is this shadow side that often portrays jealousy and has an underlying need to dominate and absorb.

It certainly became apparent way back in the time of the first Matrilineal religion. Again as history or should I say human and root race continues to repeat itself, as the saying goes a 'leopard does not change its spots'. Perhaps it is a karmic debt issue, which replays itself over and over again until there is resolution and the scales of divine justice has sought balance. However the masculine certainly did conform to form and somehow felt threatened by the power of the Mami Wata Priestesses and its religion. Even though the Sibyls, held on for over a thousand years, this was too much for the masculine to bear.

Even today in a so-called civilised age, we call forth from our hearts, "How can these events happen?" Especially while witnessing the atrocities throughout the world. As we watch in shock as our world leaders, play with fire and incompetence, lacking compassion, day after day as they mindlessly provoke and disrespect other cultures. Stupidity or lack of thought prospers in a realm where diplomacy and deference have lost their meaning. I am not sure if we are evolving correctly now, as we watch such manipulation and coercing on a transparent and wide-scale, widespread in the so-called free-world as well as in the lesser developed countries? An illusion has sprung forth from the minds of individual world leaders; one cleverly projected throughout the TV, Media and Social Media platforms. The colloquial black mirror indeed mirrors back our dark inner recesses and replays itself in our desires and the illusions we create and those projected on us.

What type of world have we created? Have you ever switched on a news channel and watched a prominent news station with the mute button on? The screen is ablaze with running captions of news straplines, always on a loop on the bottom of the screen.

Meanwhile, the news anchor is seated in front of a constant stream of violent and war-torn images. As we watch men and women whose faces contort as they portray 'their version of the truth', spouting nothing other than a continuous stream of opinions. These images of horror, death, and War paraded in front of us daily. What is this darkness we see? What manipulation are we subjected to, and yet one we are unable to stop? Is this how human life has ended up, emblazoned on a screen as we mindlessly watch these horrors unfold like robots?

Here we see man, woman and humanity portrayed in all its ugly glory; we should ask where is the light, where are the lightworkers who are here to support and put us 'the children of men' back on its moral highway. Perhaps humanity has become endemic and lost in its round of power and glory-seeking, perhaps we are nothing other than a movable chess piece, moved into position for the entertainment of the gods. An experiment to prove a divine scientific theory to show what happens to a race of people who when given choices and 'free will'. Revert to a type, whose basic aim is to ensure their survival, while in the meantime collecting as much material stuff along the way to appease their lost selves.

While this is the case, our evolution is impeded by our genetics and our ancestry, why? Because humanity is its own strapline, in a loop, generation after generation. Because the way we do things now is driven by a subconscious influence from the past, is it a ploy that allows this loop to continue? We are a sum of every myth, fairy-tale and legend, and it runs rampant within our bloodlines and proffers every sense and emotion we too offer the world.

Mami Wata, Eradicated

Let us look at what happened to the primordial Matrilineal religion, as we return to the time of Mami Wata and the Queen Mothers. Their temples, once in favour and respected as were the oracles who ran them. Offering Divine counsel to the Kings and Queens and Generals. Their mysteries were sought after, so much jealously ran through the blood of these many wannabe takers. The High Priestesses were overseen from the sidelines, as they performed and delivered their prophecies and guided the way forward to promote much-needed success in either battle or strategy. The priest/esses of Mami Wata and Sacred Divine law were the Sibyls who had a direct line of communication to the etheric realms. The word 'Sibyl' comes from a Greek word, 'Sibylla' meaning Prophetess or an oracle who under divine influence from the gods, prophesied the oracles and wrote these into manuscripts. Her practice portrays her as an older woman who muttered predictions while in transcendental fervour.

The[10] Sibyls are the descendants of the very first Neolithic clans of the African warrior queens, healers, prophets/esses on the first ship built by the Goddess, to establish a new world after the Great Flood. The Patriarchy names this as Noah and his three sons. They were African women; High Priestesses called Sybils. Two black doves flew out from the Argos (ark), the first to Thebes in Egypt, the second to Dodona Delphi, where temples were erected in both locations.

The Sibyls were prolific throughout the ancient world, some identified as being well known such as the Persian Sibyl named Sambethe, reported to be from the family of Noah, also possibly identified as the Babylonian Sibyl, presided over the Apollonian Oracle and counselled over the exploits of Alexander the Great. The Libyan Sibyl, and Oracle from Egypt, a granddaughter of Poseidon and consulted by Alexander the Great.

The Delphic Sibyl, named Themus who stems from before the Trojan wars, was also the Muse behind Michelangelo's Sistine Chapel. Gnaeus Naevius a poet and dramatist from around 201Bc to 270BC names a Cimmerian Sibyl in his books about the Punic Wars. The Erythraean Sibyl identified as being one of the 'Black Doves' sent out to find land from the ark. She predicted the Trojan War and prophesied to the Greeks who were moving against Ilium both that Troy would be destroyed, she wrote her prophecies on laurel leaves.

The Cumaean Sibyl from the Greek city of Naples was one who the Romans became most worried about; she is reported to have sold the Sibylline Books to Tarquinius the last King of Rome, who is infamous in his initial rejection of her offer, so she took some of the scrolls and burned them. Then she went back and offered the sale of them again, and again he refused, so she burned more of the manuscripts. Until one of his essential advisors told him what was in there. Hurriedly he purchased the remaining manuscripts. Here inside them contains her

----

[10] Exert from The Sybils (The First Prophesttess' of Mami Wata) by Mama Zogbe

prophecy telling of the coming of a saviour who later identified as Jesus.

The Hellespontine Sibyl from Libya or Tunisia worked in the temple of Apollo at Gergis, also known as the Trojan Sibyl who presided over the Apollonian Oracle at Dardania. The Romans added a further Sibyl known as the Tiburtine Sibyl, named Albunea, located in modern Tivoli. She was adored and worshipped as a goddess, and it was her oracles that the Senate transferred into the Capitol. She prophesies the coming of a final emperor named Constans, who would defeat the enemies of Christianity. It is from here we enter a space to identify a very divisive era. As over time, these very same written oracles would soon become stolen and usurped, repackaged and sold as something new. The last Sibyl I would like to talk about was a Hebrew Sibyl named Sabbe. Even though some researchers say she was Babylonian, some call her the Egyptian Sibyl. Sabbe was brought up in Palestine, and she remains credited as being the author of the Sibylline Oracles. A sixth-century collection of oracles that predict disasters. They say 14 books survived and are viewed by some Christians as a predictive authority equivalent to the Old Testament.

Considering this possibility, and how a comparison exists between the Oracles and the Old Testament. We should look further into what happened. As I mentioned earlier, the Sibyls were the first representations of Mami Wata and Isis, beholding an ability to communicate with the Higher Realms directly, their high ranking ensured an almost royal status and afforded them power. However, they were watched with jealous observation.

Surprisingly at this stage, it wasn't the Romans who were a threat. They depended on the prophecies and magic of the Sibyls. Surprisingly the decline of the representative of the Divine Mothers began in Egypt, as a powerful priesthood began to emerge and invade her temples. The Priests of Amun or Amen worshipped a creator god, depicted as the force which created life. However, the myths and writings tell how he helped his people become successful in victory and solving problems using oracles and how a statue of Amun could move in answer to any question posed, and this was later debunked to show how the priests would touch the figure to make it move, thus manipulating the answers. The God of Thebes, though viewed as a Primordial Creation god, was only important to the locals. The priests of Amon grew more and more powerful and wealthy and soon sought to gain influence within the political arena. Those affiliated with Amon and who requested favours from him would be asked to confess their sins first to prove their loyalty. The way of surrendering ones sins was later to become one of the principles of Catholicism.

It takes little imagination to see how the Sibyls would be seen as a threat to any aspiring male Priesthood.

The Priests of Amon began sexually abusing the once untouchable Priestesses in the Mothers temples, a despicable method used to sully the priestesses and temple maidens purity

Interestingly, it is here we witness the absolute start of demeaning the feminine, by debasing the Divine Mothers representatives inside her sacred temples, sent a patriarchal message and presented the ultimate insult to the Divine Feminine, its sole aim to devalue and degrade her.

In the same way, the Catholic religion has degraded its position in the stakes of sacred trust as it allows and is complicit, regarding its priests who reveal their inner darkness by stealing the purity of children, via the abhorrent and endemic sexual abuse.

Even though the Priests of Amon's power was seemingly short-lived in the grand scale of history, they were shortly followed by the Sons of Horus or old Osirian Religion, after much toing and froing of the lives and deaths of Pharaohs. It was Tutankhamun who was responsible for moving forward in his reign by reverting to the old religion and old Gods of Egypt as he favoured the old Osirian Gods, finally usurping the self-created god of Amon.

It was during these times that the Sibyls temples were gradually being taken from them and some Sibyls found themselves faced with a dangerous and challenging choice to make, either conform and work alongside these new regimes or become stripped of their status, murdered or to try and escape the tyranny! Many of the priestesses opted instead to end their lives rather than submit to subservience. Throughout the Ancient seats of the matrilineal religion, many competing patriarchal sects began to desire complete and utter dominion. Arising under the reign of King Menes c 2,925 BC, patriarchal control spread over the Mothers temples and shrines. (Though an important note to mention here, as some reserchers describe Menes as belonging to a Divine Lineage of Dragon Bloodlines). However, this is a story for another time.

The Sacred Python Is Slaughtered

The ultimate betrayal of all that was and the Divine feminine religion arrived in the form of the Black Hebrew Levites, or tribe of Levi as it is known. Their priestly roles are handed down from father to son. But, before I tell this story, I would like to explain, As the Divine Ancestral Mother religion had swept through much of the Ancient world. Its source was in Africa. It was powerfully guarded by the indigenous tribes. It was a female-centred religion surrounding the worship of God/Goddess and Iyami. It held autonomy by the power and magic it offered. A further point to mention was the rise of the Semitic religions centred around Patriarchal monotheism, which spread from the Ancient near-East to NE Africa. The patriarchy was vying for its autonomous reign. These included the now well-known, sects of Islam, Judaism and Christianity. But before these became the usurpers, there were rumblings in other cultures as well and who were connected by a shared belief in one masculine God. Even though the timelines are different for these other usurpers, including the Assyrians (from Babylon, Sumeria) the Canaanites (Northern Syria) the Islamic (Arabian, Saudi and Persia) and The Black Hebrew Levites.

Here, we find the ultimate betrayal funded by the Black Hebrews, who were the descendants of the nation of Israel and became known as the lost tribes who became scattered throughout Africa. The Hebrew Israelites were from the bloodline of Noah, via his son Shem and then down the family line to Terah's son Abraham, known to be dark-skinned and for being the Father of the Hebrews. Shem himself was raised in the Cushite civilisation of Ethiopia. It was later decreed that God offered land to the descendants of Abraham, located along the Nile towards the Euphrates. It was here that the sons of Jacob who was a grandson of Abraham, settled and it became where the Hebrew nation remained and resided in Egypt for 215 years.

Later on, in the tenth century BC, a dateline which includes 901 BC to 1,000 BC, the story expands. During this time, Makeda, the Queen of Sheba, visited the famed King of Solomon of Israel. She bore him a son, David Menelik, who was raised in the Kingdom of Israel by King Solomon until he was 19 years old. He was then sent by Solomon to Ethiopia accompanied by the Levite Priests, and his mission was to relocate and establish. 'The house of David' in his Fathers name. He reportedly took the coveted Ark of the Covenant to Ethiopia, which was a gold-covered chest, contained inside were the two stone tablets of the ten commandments, Aarons rod and a pot of Manna (foodstuff). The Levites used the practice of sacrifice and appeasement by offering burnt offerings, a method still alive in African religious traditions today. When King Solomon died in 925-BC, a partition of Ancient Israel happened, it was divided into the Kingdon of Israel, North Israel which today is better known as Israel, Palestine, Jordan and Syria. And the Kingdom of Judah, Southern Levant.

What transpired and actioned by the Levites was non-other than ethnic cleansing in the form of ridding the Divine Mothers temples of the Serpent-Priestesses and Sibyls. They slaughtered the iconic and symbolic Ancestral Python and replaced it with an Eagle. They forced the Priestesses to either work for the House of David or be killed. The fate of the prophetic scrolls resulted in many being burned and destroyed. Some of the leftover scrolls became the property of the Levites, who in what can only be described as a lack of cultural knowledge. Poorly translated them and placed them into the Judeo-Christian Bible, the Torah and Pentateuch.

All traces of the black gods/goddesses and her religion were wiped and repackaged and renamed, and her Priestesses were debased beyond imagination as Jezabels and pagan witches. The legacy of those times became encased in violence and war, a destruction of great magnitude. From this moment on, the role of the feminine, changes, to a far lesser, subservient and diminished role. The world is left with none other than several would-be religions whose claim of divine greatness has been based on lesser-known gods and scripture. The religious art pieces include Europeanised graphic content as do all depictions of ancient sculptures. All legitimacy of the importance of Africa and its role in the source of humanity has become dispersed. After being invaded and depreciated by the Muslims and other usurpers. Who made sure the tribe's people accepted these new self-styled religions. The African people have been subjected to fear and enslavement for centuries its foundation overlayed by a set of the invaders self-proclaimed beliefs and written law.

Those who stole the land and dominated its people were urged forward by their despicable behaviours and actions, including manipulation, lies, child abuse, violence, slavery, murder and sexual abuse. They did this, for no other reason than to steal the minerals in a mineral-rich land and for the mere pleasure of domination.

The Sacred Python Is Destroyed in Ireland Too

We can even trace this eradication of the matrilineal powers to a common western figurehead known and celebrated as Saint Patrick. I can envision him now, standing proud and aloft, as he proclaimed his infamous banishment of 'ridding Ireland of all the snakes and pushing them into the sea'.

However, truthful factors remain to exist, and this, I know.

There is in existence, a bloodline a lineage sourced from a Divinely Royal descent, it doesn't include the commonly known Royal Houses of the World. But comes directly from the Divine Ancestral Mothers of Africa, via Iyami and is inherited by blood down through its matrilineal bloodlines of descendency, it connects many Africans today as well as those incarnated into other cultures during this lifetime. The phrase, 'The secrets lie within the blood' stands firm, as it doesn't matter how many self-styled religions are proclaimed, you cannot change this fact, bloodlines are the inheritance of source. The purity of oneness is rising once more, and it will be the women who bring forth this.

Let me close this chapter with a list of patriarchal beliefs to ponder on:

Patriarchal Beliefs

- God reveals Himself as masculine, not feminine.
- God ordained distinct gender roles for man and woman as part of the created order.
- A husband and father is the head of his household, a family leader, provider, and protector.
- Male leadership in the home carries over into the church: only men are permitted to hold ruling positions in the church. A God-honouring society will likewise prefer male leadership in civil and other spheres.

- Since the woman was created as a helper to her husband, as the bearer of children, and as a 'keeper at home', the God-ordained and proper sphere of dominion for a wife is the household and that which relates to the home.
- God's command to 'be fruitful and multiply' still applies to married couples.
- Christian parents must provide their children with a thoroughly Christian education, one that teaches the Bible and a biblical view of God and the world.
- Both sons and daughters are under the command of their fathers if they are under his roof or otherwise, the recipients of his provision and protection.

Chapter 6
Impressions of Karma

What is karma? It is a river running deep within the souls catalogue of previous earth-life experiences. Each experience has an impact on a souls journey from its beginning and onwards through the ages. Imprints made from the actions and behaviours we create, dependent on the circumstances of the event are held within the deepest part of our souls subconscious. A river that meanders through time, throughout the streams of consciousnesses. A continuous and ever-present catalogue of 'how we lived'. All held in the halls and libraries of the ever-after. Many instances of good, bad and the downright ugly all end up in a personal accountability bank. Where several good deeds will cancel out lesser impactive immoral acts. It is the downright ugly deeds, which create a much more profound and engraved imprint, all held in the record of our spirit. We are urged to always 'stay in the light' and not to allow the shadows to invade and claim us if they do, then we could head down a path of self-destruction and even worse, become a danger to others. Self-sabotage is a more indicative purveyor of self-harm and denial of life itself. Readily sought and an easy target when life provides many of its more negative and troublesome experiences. A path, full of crossroads and dead endings will soon batter the physical and mental bodies of a person, one which offers admirable courage of resistance to moving forward from these endemic places.

Patterning

There is a caveat, or perhaps it is better explained as a possible reason for accumulating karma in the first place. Maybe this is due to the very origin of humanity, one from an earlier root race. Whereby we have lost all sense of connection and being part of the original purity and oneness. Is it fair to say we have lost our way, fallen from grace, thrown out of the Garden of Eden, to fend for ourselves? Man against man, dog eats dog etc. We are lost as we meander throughout lifetimes, looking for the perfect life, home and experiences. Yet, whatever we do, something or someone comes into the mix and offers up a challenging life event.

To elaborate and to offer a reason for why things happen and why we seem to be trapped in a seemingly energetic jail of stuckness. I provide you with a bigger picture, as a way, to explain this disconnection from purity.

Incorruptible Purity

In the beginning, Divine consciousness created the planets and galaxies. Sending its emissaries, Iyami to seed life on Earth. Throughout these excursions and it has happened in various forms, as per the root race scenario. Amidst this creation, the Creative principle, commanded the Pantheons of Deities to support, watch over and teach human life to survive. These Deities were known as the Orishas in African cosmology.

Who Are the Orishas?

There are 401 Orisha names known in the Yoruba Pantheon. The ancient mythology of the Yoruba people is a significant religion in Nigeria, claimed by its followers to be one of the oldest religions in the world and still practised today. It has since brought forth new, modified world religions such as Santería in Cuba and Candomblé in Brazil.

The Yoruba are a people of fertile soil and full of mystery, the Yoruba people of Nigeria dance to the beats of the Batá drum under the moonlight, chanting away to the Mother goddess, offering their gratitude to Oduduwa, the godfather of the land—this is a tribe with a story, and it is one which is sourced from Mami Wata, though Mami Wata is not known to be Orisha.

The Orishas are deities that reflect the manifestations of Olodumare (The Most-High God). They are emissaries of God, and they are the forces of nature. There are no images of any Orisha because they are aspects of life and are therefore energetic. For ease of understanding, because of reasonable limitation of the mind and because imagery projects reality, which in turn can constrict our beliefs, you will sometimes see illustrative portrayals of these deities, though, within their shrines in Africa, you will never find this.

Every human manifests an attribute of these natural forces within their consciousness, therefore showing knowingly or unknowingly which Orisha is their guardian. In other words, we are all children of the Orishas.

[11]A List of Some of the Orishas

Elegba

Elegba (also referred to as Eleggua or Elegguá) is the owner of the roads and doors in this world. He is the repository of ashé. Elegba stands at the crossroads of the human and the divine, as he is a child-like messenger between the two worlds.

Ogún

Ogún is the god of iron, war and labour. He is the owner of all technology, and because of this technology shares in his nature, it is almost always used first for war.

---

[11] Sourced from https://www.cs.indiana.edu

Oshosi

Oshosi is the third member of the group known as the Warriors and is received along with Elegba, Ogún and Osun to protect the warrior initiate and to open and clear their roads. Oshosi is the hunter and the scout of the orishas and assumes the role of translator for Obatalá with whom he has a very close relationship.

Obatalá

Obatalá is the kindly father of all the orishas and all humanity. He is also the owner of all heads and the mind. Though it was Olorun who created the universe, it is Obatalá who is the creator of the world and humanity. Obatalá is the source of all that is pure, wise, peaceful and compassionate. He has a warrior side though through which he enforces justice in the world.

Oyá

Oyá is the ruler of the winds, the whirlwind and the gates of the cemetery. Her number is nine which recalls her title of Yansa or 'Mother of Nine' in which she rules over the Egun or dead.

Oshún

Oshún rules over the sweet waters of the world, the brooks, streams and rivers, embodying love, fertility. She also is the one we most often approach to aid us in money matters. She is the youngest of the female orishas but retains the title of Iyalode or great queen. She heals with her sweet waters and with honey which she also owns.

Yemayá

Yemayá lives and rules over the seas and lakes. She also rules over maternity in our lives as she is the Mother of All. Her name, a shortened version of Yeyé Omo Eja means 'Mother Whose Children are the Fish' to reflect the fact that her children are uncountable. All life started in the sea, the amniotic fluid inside the mother's womb is a form of the sea where the embryo must transform and evolve through a type of fish before becoming a human baby.

Olokun

The source of all riches which he/she freely gives to her little sister Oshún. Dressing in seven skirts of blue and white and like the seas and deep lakes she is sincere and unknowable. In her path of Okutti, she is the queen of witches carrying within her deep and dark secrets.

Shangó

Perhaps the most 'popular' of the orishas, Shangó rules over lightning, thunder, fire, the drums and dance. He is a warrior orisha with quick wits, quick temper and is the epitome of masculinity. Shangó took the form of the fourth Alaafin (supreme king) of Oyó on Earth for a time. He is an extraordinarily hot-blooded and strong-willed orisha.

Orunmila

Orunmila is the Orisha of wisdom and divination. He was the only orisha allowed to witness the creation of the universe by Olorun and bears witness to our destinies in the making as well. It is the source of his title of Eleri Ipin or 'Witness to Destiny in its Creation'. His priests, the Babalawos or 'Fathers of the Secrets' must devote themselves entirely to the practice of divination and the accompanying arts.

Let us note, all female Orishas are part of the Iyami Pantheon.

The Overlayed Patterns

There was once a purity of oneness in the world and now it is lost,. However lost it has become, this could be down to the actions of each root race, and it is due to the consequences of these actions each root race took. There is, however, one source we can genuinely understand, and this comes after the first religion or when the feminine was usurped and denounced. Again, we should look at the underlying influences of the patriarchal seizing of the reigns of power.

We can pinpoint the origin of patriarchy between the period of 8,000 and 3,000 BC when early agriculture yielded a surplus, and the beginnings of militarisation helped the masculine seize control of the excess as well as being the leading producers of labour and power. The step away from a belief in a pantheon of Goddesses and Gods was brought about by a need to take advantage of the degeneration of control and autonomy over religion, which as we now know was at the time held by the Queen Mothers. The Patriarchy wanted to build a new relationship that was not dependent on Deities and Angelic mediators, and it is here Monotheism, was born.

What Does It Mean to Have Patriarchal/Human Control?

It means that the divine consciousness becomes contained in a belief in one masculine god.

Divine consciousness is sub-divided into three main religions.

Islam, Christianity and Judaism

- Each Religion creates its filters in the guise of Angelic Beings and Deities.
- The Deities, over time, become more and more human-like in both reference and accessibility.
- Each Religions rituals, focus on supremacy over the other religions, to reaffirm its power in the world.
- The result proffers disharmony, imbalance and destruction, wars, and violence ensues
- Dogma becomes controlling and invokes strong emotions.

- Subdivision causes consciousness to be weakened as the power becomes diluted.
- The religious system soon becomes degenerated, and human-made, leaving an empty container, for parasitical beings and weak humans to step in.
- Parasitical entities move into religion and operate throughout the Priesthoods.
- Priesthoods, soon adopt God-like personas, believing they can create deities and destabilise the Divine process due to their self-imposed importance.
- Priesthoods become, hierarchical in power and riches
- Priesthoods are also Sainted and are worshipped as Deities.

Corruptible

Once power takes form and becomes exteriorised and moulded. The potential for corruption is vastly increased. Add humanity to this, and then it becomes overwhelming. In religions around the world, both then and now. We witness this corruptible power at play and the evidence of predatory beings moving in. The purity of Divine Consciousness becomes the folly of man's inner weakness and desires. As obsession, manipulation and brainwashing are rife throughout the worlds Priesthoods and the religions they serve:

Here are a few examples of corruption in religion

India – Hindu philosophy suggests living a simple life, the self-proclaimed Godmen and Gurus have accumulated wealth and live a lavish life-style. Well educated people follow them to make them further rich. Money is power, and influential people may not have a conscience, in which case allows the possibility of corruption to breed.

Muslims in the Arab World – entirely male dominated; women still secondary with little or no voice.

Voodoo – reformed, for survival and a need for justice due to the diaspora from the slave trade, however, the system is significantly flawed, with requests for high payments for services. There is also the risk of non-initiates offering rituals etc.

Catholicism – Male priesthood, lead the peoples' spiritual welfare along with enforcing masculine laws. Its Priests are forbidden to marry, which causes sexual urges and immoral behaviour. Such restriction within the female Convent side, after vows of poverty, chastity and obedience are taken, promotes cruelty, obsession and frustration.

Christianity, especially in the USA, provides obsessive rhetoric-based religious ideals and laws, used to excuse human behaviours, rather than allowing accountability for ones actions.

Judaism – Though a keeper of the great mysteries, it is a religion that is belied by past suffering, a fear of extermination and proffers elitism.

Scientology – Run on the money it requests from its members, based around rigid human-made laws, taken from the beliefs of an American author who wrote about science fiction fantasies.

Amish – Rigid rules archaic beliefs, centred around a male-dominated hierarchy. Women have little power. Even in dress and ability.

Baptists – Mainly in the USA, a religion forced on the diaspora due to the Slave Trade, now fervent in worship, created as a distraction from suffering. It has replaced the old Vodoun and latter Voodoo religions.

Incorruptible Is Now Corruptible

When you view purity coming from a source of oneness, you look to see where it has gone? Whatever form we had first tasted it, has now become locked under a pattern of corruptibility. An analogy is like looking at a pure white rabbit with beautifully soft fur and covering it in a toxic purple dye. Or in more human terms, taking the purity of a child and imbuing him with social and educational constructs. We seem to want to destroy, corrupt and mar all things of virtue.

Due to the need of the masculine to seek, conquer, dominate and create his laws and edicts. This has resulted in a newly created patterning, like a dark web that is spread across the lands of the world. Man himself has overlaid and hidden the purity of natural law. Instead, he has marked his territory with toxic excrement, as a way to claim and control. Even the religions he stole, have been reformed into his rhetoric, hence the fact, most of the worlds known beliefs are human-made.

Perhaps a further analogy would be to look at the first conquering nations, the Vikings, The Romans and the Normans. How their obsession with plunder and domination, took them from their lands, marching or sailing into the territories of others, to ensure their wealth and power. Eventually, colonising many countries and building their structures, castles and churches. The invaders have not only come in to dominate the indigenous people of the land. But also, to embed their foreign patterns onto the captured areas. It has occurred mainly through human-made religions, whereby these patterns have become overlaid on sacred power sources and etched into place via erecting a building and charging its physical structures.

Foreign patterns, whether in the physical structures, such as Churches, Government Buildings, Law Courts, Temple Spaces and Multinational Companies. Were put in place to magically mark their territories and contain their dominant power and greed. No different than a dog who pees to leave its scent, the reason is to ensure it wards off those who want to take its power or infiltrate.

The outcome here as well in other countries is that the natural flow of original sacred powers within a landmass, for example, Mother Ireland, her life-giving Elements, Her Guardians, Gods and Goddesses and their helpers in physical form like the Druids. Remain stuck beneath a foreign patterning or have been forced to leave Ireland altogether. Every country should, therefore, try to return to their natural sacred power and purity, by removing the foreign patterns and bringing back sovereignty to their country once more.

Alternative Spiritual Practice Is Affected

Those who seek out alternative spiritual paths and yearn to return to its pure roots and wisdom teachings will be disappointed to discover, this: unless they seek the reliable source of their chosen spiritual path, whether it is in Shamanism, Freemasonry, Paganism, Druidry, Magic etc., you will not find it, because the farthest back you will be able to learn from. Is to the last foreign pattern imprinted across its land. Nowadays all teachings and practices offered by teachers (unless they teach from the real source) are drawn from the last in situ colonisation, this now begins the 'Neo-alternative'. The formal rituals used and overlayed power surges imprinted. The buildings they erected whether a temple or a church, the current priesthoods using their magic and rituals, have created and imprinted its colonial patterning and therefore encased the natural and pure flow of the original land. Christianity is an excellent example of how an unfamiliar pattern has concealed an ancient sacred power.

Let us now look at other influences, which can commandeer our energy and life-force.

The Karmic Shadow

How easy it is to become consumed by the 'shadow' when you haven't enough money to live on or love eludes you, or you lose the ones you love. Sickness and dis-ease are also catalysts, which may head one into these dark places. There are times when even the smallest crack of light isn't enough to offer a break from a living purgatory, and many find themselves, sinking into an inevitable void.

Choices and free will are offered at every turn of our journey, as we dodge and weave through the annals of our life. Hesitance and a longing for a road less complicated will become the backbone of a choice made or a decision acted upon. Sometimes, life has battered an already weary soul into submission, where the opportunities are seemingly scarce, and we see a break in the darkness. Thinking this must be the long-awaited gift from the universe, so readily we jump in, to find, our decision doesn't come without conditions, a price must be paid. The archetypal piper must be paid. How do we ever know whether a choice made is the right path to take for our salvation. Why is there always an ebb and a flow? Why is there a gift followed shortly by a fall? One hand giveth, and the other hand takes it away, what sort of banking system is this?

Let us return to the subject of karma, looking back through the records of our lifetimes and experiences. Upon our death we pass from the physical state into the next environment. We spend our time recapitulating our lifestream, examining our years lived on earth. How we were, what we did, how a situation turned out, how often we hurt another living being, and what happened as a consequence etc, it all requires understanding and acknowledging.

Here we balance and clear the books of karmic dross, as long as there is enough good karma to do so. When a deficit occurs and after we spend time an allotted amount of time in the otherworld, we await a situation where a requisite parentage can offer the chance to balance our soul record from the previous lifetime. When the exact and timely circumstances are made available we can drop into a new life, and we are offered a proverbial yet ethereal hall-pass. We jump eagerly, into the bright rays of a new stream and consciousness. Back into physical form and back into life, where all traces of previous lives have been wiped from memory, like cleaning the hard drive of our inner realms computer bank. We grow, we live, we experience, we become victims, saints and martyrs. Then the endemic choices arise to offer us a chance, to repair karmic accumulation or to learn the necessary lessons, that are deposited into our karmic bank vault. In addition to this, we become faced once again, with something which seems to be a continuous loop, an indicative round of choices and decisions. We ponder the thought, is there ever the right option? Do we really have captaincy over our decision making?

We dither and dawdle, we pursue, and we analyse, we pontificate, and we procrastinate. 'The decision is too hard', or 'I can't trust myself to make the right choice', or 'I can't decide what to do, let me phone a friend'. So many scenarios to consider so much toing and froing of fear and indecion. It's like entering the biggest cake shop in the world, faced with the most delicious array of sweet treats on offer. The consequences are too much even to consider. Perhaps this is the problem, choices and decisions have consequences. Not only is one more favourable than another, but every decision made will set off a ripple towards an outcome. But we have to clear these streams, to allow our lives to flow more naturally and with fewer problems,

It is true to say the word 'karma' carries with it an expression of fear and superstition. It comes with both invisible baggage and memories that underpin our day to day lives. Though they become apparent and expressed In our behaviours, addictions and actions. It becomes the force behind our communications and is the archetypal third wheel in our relationships. Truthfully it is the architect of our experiences, good and bad. Present in the events we invite in or in those that barge their way in without invite or request.

The pervasive question is 'where is all this karmic dross housed'?

Probing the physicality of our beings, we know we have a skeletal structure, comprised of bone which holds and protects our organs, tissues, and muscles. We know because we can feel it and we have seen pictures of the human body. This structure is covered with muscle fascia, a substance of collagen, to keep everything protected and in place. We have a network of neural pathways that stretch the length and breadth of our bodies, and a brain to help us both rationalise and to improve the motor function of our bodies. Beneath all of this, we are made up of a profusion of cells, all utilising and performing many tasks. We can also receive and emit frequencies, sending messages out to our nervous systems. These cells also house our DNA, the hidden knowledge regarding our inheritance and our genetic makeup.

DNA holds the imprint of where our ancestors began their lives and their ongoing migratory routes. It is a catalogue that contains so much information, regarding humanities, first learned abilities, those needed to help us survive and provide us our growth. Knowledge of a common ancestor befits the profile of all of the humans today, and it is the profile of Neanderthal Man. The first neanderthal came from Africa and became one of the early scientific discoveries. Neanderthal DNA is present in nearly 99% of the population on earth today. However, a question begs to be discussed, and this is, What is in the remaining 1% of missing DNA and where does it come from?

Recently there has been a surprising twist in the discovery, and a clue to this is found way back in time to around 500,000 and 800,000 years ago. Scientists have found no evidence of any Neanderthal DNA present in this very early African DNA. Adding more intrigue to this discovery, the scientists have identified a group of beings who lived in Africa who were wholly autonomous, without any human/neanderthal DNA. These particular people were located in the areas of Central and West Africa, and they bred with the Neanderthals. It may surprise you to know that it is this specific group from Africa who cannot be identified to any branch of the human gene pool, this indeed is a puzzle to ponder. Perhaps this adds more evidence to the fact of how such an early human could have evolved from an even older or mysterious ancestor? Maybe this is how the Ancient ancestral mothers, who came from the stars, seeded humanity, enabling us as a species to evolve towards becoming organised societies.

A further essential part of the karmic puzzle is to try and explain how karma is weighed in both the world of reality and the higher realms. There is a flip side to this coin! And that is to see how the karmic load of specific individuals impacts society when they are in physical form. Those who create disorder and mayhem in the world, whether by being violent or by taking life, can expect to hold a hefty karmic load. When these souls return to the next environment, we should contemplate a fact that these individuals never clear their karmic debts. I could add further and say they have no interest in removing it either. For certain energies, choose to continue to reside in the realm of shadow, lifetime after lifetime. Coming into physical form with one thing in mind, and this is to create and become partisan to disorder and chaos. The more of this they produce, the more it feeds their shadow tendencies. Instead, they incarnate under the guise of the 'dark'. Perhaps, and please do excuse the analogy, but look at humanity as being a representation of a scale from white to black (including a measure of fifty shades of grey). Each and everyone can be placed somewhere along this range of measurement. However, for many, there is a very good chance to clear and learn; for others, each lifetime becomes more complicated than the last, due to an inability to realise or learn. For fewer people, they can enjoy their evolutionary process as they consciously learn the lessons and ensure their physical lives are lived, accumulating as much positive karma as possible.

The Earth and its countless centuries of existence can only hold a certain amount of karma which is contained by its citizens. Otherwise if too much is present at any one time. Then the Earth cannot merely sustain the weight and denseness. If the latter happened, then I feel we would experience an apocalyptic dystopian world, one where the Shadow armies have ultimate command over. With unabridged violence and unspeakable horrors, food and water shortages and with human suffering abound on a grand scale. Before long, Earth our Mother, would step in and wipe out all trace of humans from her belly. For this reason, karma is managed by the Divine Lords of Karma and Justice, and only so much is allowed through in any given earth time frame. Even if an individual has a lot of karma to clear, they would not necessarily be allowed through until there is opportunity on earth to accommodate it.

How Do We Identify Our Karmic Debris?

If we admit and make it our responsibility for clearing karma, then we need some help and guidance. Firstly we need to find the commonality of events and experiences we have had in our lives so far, and we begin to do this by looking at the state of our subconscious river, we then begin to examine the flow of our lives. The way we do this is to recapitulate the events and experiences we have had through life. It will indicate or allude to the karma that swims along in the deep undercurrent. The best way to achieve this is by undertaking a personal recapitulation or life review. Get a journal and work through the following questions.

- What experiences have you had in life, which err on the side of unfavorable experiences which repeats throughout a specified time period? E.g Relationships, work issues, misfortune, illnesses, accidents.
- Do you meet people who are naturally deceptive or manipulative?
- Have you experienced a common trend in physical health for yourself or your bloodline?
- Do you have some strange or unexplainable fears?
- Have you had an unexplainable dislike for a parent or gender or figurehead?
- Do you often experience periods of bad luck or misfortune?
- Do you tend to be in the company of, or in a relationship with those who are violent?
- Have you a tendency to unexplained depressive or anxious behaviours?

- Do you have negative or damaging thoughts, or are you involved in criminal behaviour?
- Do you have an addictive personality?
- Do you have extreme bouts of emotions or hazardous behaviours?
- Do you regularly find yourself in dangerous environments or situations?
- Do you seek to live on a knife-edge, or are you a persistent thrill-seeker?
- Have any of your family members or ancestors been involved in dark arts or criminal behaviour?

This personal life review can help you discover karmic baggage to a degree, though it is better found when there are precise and repetitive experiences occurring. Karmic baggage isn't always readily identifiable, yet if you experience extreme types of behavioural reactions, especially those which involve any of the above indicators. It is a good indication you have some karmic baggage to attend to in your lifetime. There is always a well laid out set of clues to help you identify what needs to be cleared or healed. However, if you suspect, karmic accumulation is a problem or it is the reason for having an ongoing and challenging life. I urge you to seek help from a Shamanic professional, one who has received initiation, which allows them to carry out this function correctly,using formal processes in a ceremony.

The Karmic River

If left uncleaned, these karmic rivers run amok with debris which can sometimes cause problems further down the line. These could involve certain behavioural tendencies, or a continual run of bad luck or self-sabotage, naming a few problematic examples. When these are left unattended it will only lead one way. Perhaps manifesting as a physical or mental illness, Life-style instability where you find yourself with your back up against a wall, therefore it is well worth seeking help and guidance.

We have all read or watched the film by Dickens called 'A Christmas Carol'. The story of Ebenezer Scrooge, a dislikeable character set in the ambient era of the Victorian Age. He was an unhappy man who worked as an accountant/debt collector. He only cared about the material world and his most treasured possession: money. Because of his inner turmoil and unhappiness, he ensured his staff, including none other than the poorly victimised, Bob Cratchit, experienced a life of meanness, misery, and ongoing bullying. It wasn't until Scrooge was forced to take a look at his past, present, and future did he become a far gentler, kinder man. This well-known tale by Dickens could be used to explain the effects of karma in simplistic terms. If we recapitulate our life, to determine the person we have become. And examine our relationships, our beliefs, our actions, and our emotions, and how we are in the eyes of those closest to us. We may begin to understand the debris we have carelessly tossed like garbage into our inner rivers.

Karmic baggage not only influences our lives as becoming a collection of poorly misjudged events that causes us to employ certain negative behaviours. In the same way, it is also about the continuum or accumulation of who we are as an individual soul. Our inner rivers become a continuous flow or in some cases, a tsunami, littered with the imprints we have left unattended, lifetime after lifetime.

I always remember my teacher Dr Alberto Villoldo, talk about the importance of walking without leaving footprints behind us. I never really understood the deeper meaning of this statement. Until I began to see, many clients arrive for healing. Some of whom required having their karmic accumulation cleansed, healed or cleared.

I want to impress how essential it is to do this because to take on physical form lifetime after lifetime, would allow us to focus more on our evolution, and how this could spread out like a ripple adding to humanities more significant growth. Rather than having to focus each lifetime towards figuring out what is wrong with us? Trying to heal our ancestry, or trying to be able to right the many wrongs committed in past lives.

After all, isn't the first rule of nature, to conserve energy, well there must be a tonne of power wasted every time we need to heal or cleanse something from the past.

"Don't put off until tomorrow, what you can do today."
Benjamin Franklin

Chapter 7

Elements of Elemental Forces of Creation

"Iyami is one with the core of the Earth, and with the celestial realm, they are the lineage of the ancients. At the seeding of the core Iyami, water and earth were created at the same time, then fire and air were made manifest, immediately after to maintain balance and peace. Original Matriarchal souls gathered from our galaxy to govern the elements. Earth Mothers were already in place, and they summoned, Water Matriarchs from Sirius, known by the Dogon tribespeople as Nommos. To imbue the wisdom of water to some of the Earth Mothers from the first core, who then became Mothers of Water, called Mami Wata, Water Deities. This is a lineage that works through Olokun and Yemoja.

At the core of the Earth, Olokun, the ruler of the sea and Onile, The Earth Mother, lived side by side, they are sisters from the same core, except Olokun has more Sirian DNA. They occupy adjoining palaces, where they rule from the core of the Earth. One palace is filled with glorious gems, and the other palace is filled with sacred sparkles of water. These palaces are known as the Sacred home of the Earth and the Sea. It is the prototype of the Greek concept of Elysium and the Tibetan Shamballa.

They work to bring Divine Justice and Grace and are the affiliates of the Karmic board. All the Iyami are Mothers, and they are Super Creator Goddesses, a primal lineage of ancients, made of God and some of the stars, older than humans by Aeons."

Crystalle Ariel

Aspects of chemistry that, when mixed and infused together, will create tremendous and amazing changes and forms. Out of these factors, an alchemical manifestation of form emerges to generate objects, life and circumstances. Science has the onus on the whys and wherefores of how this happens, and I am not going to even try and match knowledge as such. Though like making a delicious meal or mixing paint on a palette, changes and miracles can occur. Essential elements of chemistry include those fundamental elements we all learned in school. Carbon, hydrogen, oxygen and nitrogen, Here, I would offer a more intimate association with the components of the natural order: fire, air, water, earth and space the ultimate building blocks of creation. The primordial and vital beginning of the Tree of Life. Its story and legacy are found in the stories of Adam and Eve and the infamous Garden of Eden. The paradise we as humanity were serendipitously thrown out of after Eve, committed the original sin. The tree of life represents a supernatural provision of ongoing growth, as long as we do not dare to eat the fruits of disobedience and gain knowledge from it. Because if we do dare, we will continue to be banished from the garden of Eden, which is the Kingdom of God. Its mention in the bible is at times ambiguous, begging more information of a further meaning, possibly this is to throw us the inquisitive humans off the scent.

Furthermore, it is written in the scriptures about the existence of two trees, the tree of life and the tree of knowledge and within this became a test, a necessary choice for Adam and Eve to make. The trial brought in the influence of choosing right over evil, a selection of obeying or disobeying. The ending, of course, is legendary, as Eve decided to leave the protection of God and the Garden of Eden, in choosing to eat the fruit of the Tree of knowledge, synonymous with choosing Satan! Both Adam and Eve, became banished, Eve because she disobeyed God (strike 1) and because she defied her consort, Adam (strike 2).

The tree of life, however, has a fuller meaning and is explained better by Gnostic and Esoteric teachings. Due to a fact of knowledge of which demonstrates our physical world is far more complicated to understand and how the laws of the Universe can offer a comprehensive understanding of the many dimensions and levels of existence which prevail outside of the world of physical reality. Here we can be advised of how the many aspects and realms of existence could influence and create further structures of existence, for example, life on earth, guided by the hands of a higher more advanced group of beings. The tree of life now becomes more synonymous with a Cosmic, Tree of life, which became manifested in the heavens first, then into the lower dimensions of existence, second. Yet it is possible to discover; these manifested worlds may only exist temporarily throughout the stages of the great eras, known both as helpful facts contained in history or as myths.

Additionally, the planet of Earth was created from the emptiness or void, from out of the darkness, the light made a manifest form, using the elements or forces of elemental creation. From out of the heavens, other dimensions exist, from the realms of apparent non-existence to the existence of physical reality – Earth. Then further replication of our planet became manifest as life or the seeds of human life became born. The teachings of the Tree of life is then transported to grow a tree of knowledge, which beholds the secret of humanities evolution and existence here on earth. After this detail, we can verify how many traditions from all around the world and how these civilisations represent the tree of life as being a significant source of knowledge, divine truth and logos of 'who we are' and 'where we came from'.

The tree of life is associated with the Original Mothers, the Serpent (or so-called temptress, who lured poor Eve away into the realms of disobedience) Then again, perhaps humanities fall from grace should be better termed as an ongoing sacrifice to develop our spiritual natures further. Numerous civilisations mention the Tree of Life as an essential symbol of their beliefs, from the Assyrians (Source Ancient Mesopotamia) later Syria, and now Iraq. To Buddha who was born under the Bodhi tree and who found enlightenment under this sacred tree. The Egyptians revered the sycamore tree associated with the Goddess Nut (Divine Mother), The Greek Tree of life is depicted as being found in the Garden of the Hesperides, which is a grove of golden apple trees belonging to the Goddess Hera, when eaten would grant immortality to he/she who ate them. Again it is the serpent who guarded these apple trees.

Furthermore, trees of life are associated with the Olmecs who were an early civilisation in Mexico and the Ancient Mayans, who depicted the tree of life as the three levels of life, the underworld, the physical world of reality (Earth) and the Heavens. Famously the Nordic tree of life known in Norse mythology as Yggdrasil which was a large ash tree of which held the nine realms of the cosmos. The Yggdrasil supported all of creation from the Gods to giants, humanity and animals.

The Tibetan tree of life is represented in the Sanskrit work Kalachakra which means wheel of time and is found in all the Tibetan Buddhist traditions and appertains to the Universal laws and structures of which manage existence and its mystical teachings.

The role of the serpent as the protector, played further in the Feminine Religion of Mami Wata, as these Serpent Priestesses, guarded the scrolls and prophecies and communications with the Divine truth, fervently. In many traditions, the Serpent is known as the Mother of Waters, and the Tree of Life. However, there is a further lesser-known association. It is the Legend and existence of Lemuria or Mu, the Mother of Humanity and the only source or beginning of life. The creation story is communicated further here, and it relates to Lemuria first birthing of existence in the Universe. Remember Lemuria was the third root race!

In the beginning, the Universe, comprised only a soul and spirit. An endless void where everything was without form and life was non-existent. In the dense blackness of this emptiness, all was serene, silent and without audio. Space itself was immense, and the void was lost in its darkness. The Supreme Being, the Creatrix, was the only movement to be found in the endemic dark. In a moment s/he wanted to create Earth, and on its surface s/he decided to place life, humans and animal life forms. The Creatrix ushered seven commands. The first command 'Let the gases, which are scattered throughout space and without structure and order, be brought together and out of these allow worlds to form.

The gases came together in the form of whirling masses. The gases solidified, leaving some on the outside of the earth's crust The second command was 'let the gases separate and let the waters and atmosphere be formed'. From this waters and atmosphere formed and volumes remained contained within the crust. The gases formed into the water and covered the Earth and the remainder created the atmosphere, which gave birth to light. Then the shafts of the sun met the beams of the Earths heat, which was contained in her atmosphere, and it gave it life. When there was heat to warm the face of the earth. The fourth command was. Let the fires that are within the planet raise the land above the face of the waters. Then the flames of the underneath lifted the ground on which the waters rested until the land appeared above the front of the seas; this was the dry land.

The fifth command was, Let life come forth from the waters, and the shafts of the sun met the beams of the earth in the mud of the seas and out of the particles, clay formed cosmic eggs, and from these eggs, life came forth as commanded. The sixth command was, let life come forth on the land, And the beams of the sun met the shafts of the earth in the dust of the ground and out of particles of dust formed cosmic eggs. From these cosmic eggs, life came forth as commanded. The seventh command: And when this was done, the seventh intellect said, let us make man after our fashion and let us endow him with powers to rule the earth. The Creatrix of all things throughout the universe created man and placed him on his body, a living imperishable spirit and man became like the Creatrix in intellectual power.

"Exert from the third book in James Churchward's Mu series, one of several which slipped into the public domain in the US because some paperwork wasn't submitted in time to the copyright office. This one seemed to be the most on-topic for this site.

Churchward served in the British Army for thirty years. He claimed that, while posted in India, he befriended a priest ('Rishi'), who revealed to him ancient tablets written in an otherwise unknown language. The Rishi taught Churchward how to read this language, Naacal. The tablets described the land of Mu, the Lemuria of the Theosophists. He also claimed that he was able to discern writing from Mu on a mysterious set of tablets discovered in Mexico by an explorer named William Niven.

Churchward's Mu theory hasn't achieved even the marginal credibility of Atlantis. For one thing, his science is absurd. The Pacific appears to have been free of large landmasses for billions of years. The Pacific basin may mark the place where the Moon was expelled from the proto-earth. Coral atolls that dot the Pacific have taken millions of undisturbed years of activity to form. And the Pacific was one of the last regions on the planet to be settled by humans; this is proven by scientific evidence and the well-documented oral traditions which describe the history of the Polynesian migrations."

To understand such ancient myths and texts which relate to a time beyond anything we could have known seems absurd when trying to contemplate a vision of how it was back then. Yet we have become marginalised in our knowledge processes and cleverly confined in a patriarchal worldview of a seemingly modern perspective of events. Our timeline is narrow because his story has been condensed in a small window and timeline, compiled by a small number of scribes, religious recorders and historians. As I have said often, so much has been destroyed and lost, so much has become manipulated and even much more information about what happened has been hidden from us.

Therefore so much is seemingly a hypothesis of what could have been, as we await the general premise and scientific proof, to validate all the sacred information, which many seers and prophets already knew. Though I remind you, we do hold all of the attributes of every myth, fairy story and legend within our DNA. At one time, we experienced these previous root races.

I guess we should always ask the question, why, so many of us have been given such information and have spent lifetimes in proving such facts of ostensible fantasy did exist. How and why are there so many people obsessively trying to validate knowledge of the existence of Atlantis and Lemuria? After all, there is such a large percentage of people who still believe in the presence of a God and Jesus Christ, Mohammed, Buddha, Mother Mary, Saints and Archangels. Belief in esoteric form does, after all, become the fundamental basis of most religious holy works. Yet to talk about Iyami, the Divine Mothers or even a time beyond a certain point in Ancient history becomes imprecise and unbelievable. Thousands of people all over the world still attend holy temples and churches and pray, for forgiveness, relief and a better way of life, week after week in their prayers. Infusing a belief in something far more significant than themselves to get the help they seek. However, to reinstall a Matriarchal system of canonical form, for many seems to be an impertinent and irreverent ideal. It would imply a supposition of acceptance and denial of feminine ability in a sacred figurehead role. Perhaps it is because the feminine has endured lifetimes of subjugation and suppression, women no longer have the ability to fight their way back from behind the kitchen sink?

Perhaps the very idea of any existence of the continents of Lemuria and Atlantis, holding the hypothesis of power, evolution as well as a celebration of a sacred way of life, indeed has become forged in the annals of myth and fantasy? Or is it an available train of thought to infer, Lemuria and Atlantis were earlier or the original experiments involving human existence? One which merely down to type due to greed and a need for more and more power, caused the Most High to literally sink these Islands, due to offending and upsetting God or the Creator? By now you must realise we are a hares breath away from annihilation and extinction? I can fully imagine the 'All that is' with their finger hovering over the 'end of days' button. Waiting in anticipation for someone to have the sense to stop the insanity and retrieve the balance. Or thinking to themselves, "Let us kick off version 6 and get the 6th Root Race-ready."

If we are to consider these early civilisations as a previous form of humanity, then perhaps we should think about why they no longer exist. Mainly when there was so much evidence of a perfect society and a vibrant existence of trade, magic and wellbeing all awhile living alongside, different planetary star seeds. Then we should ask, what went wrong when we assume, these societies had everything they required? Looking back at these civilisations, one could imagine from the viewpoint of today, it was indeed utopia. If we focus on an imprecise hypothesis of life, then, perhaps we can overlay global information now and make some assumptions as to what went wrong. Let us look at the demise of these islands and work forward from there.

The information can indeed be debated because there is no factual evidence of what happened, only assumptions and these are backed up with the insights of modern-day prophetesses. Regarding a mythical explanation and as all good myths explain, there is both a warning and prophecy which comes from any ancient fictitious story.

The islands of Lemuria were where the Iyami first came as Super-Goddesses, who were charged with interacting with humanity to bring forth divine justice and love. These Goddesses became a bridge between the Cosmos and Earth. Their role was to bring the edicts from the Highest God to the citizens of Earth. Allowing humanity to build and live from their heart. If anything went wrong, then the Goddesses would bring justice to bring forth balance and harmony once more. Humankind during these times was not built from the same vein as humans today. Many had access to magical powers and gifts, enforced and enhanced from living alongside star-seeds. Building and erecting was a much more magical task than using brawn and planning as we do today. Instead, buildings were constructed using advanced tools and abilities. Life on Lemuria and Atlantis coincided with sacred law and order as well as the use of superior skills.

Significantly to concur here is to look at how the modern-day templates of Adam and Eve today, require a need to be known and to make their mark as a measure of their existence. Humankind now and way back then have possibly not evolved too differently. It seems, to say there can never be enough riches, power or notoriety, for humans to have. Look around the globe today and how those in power, or those who hold the balance of industry at their fingertips act. Especially if threatened with challengers or the fear of losing their business. I would think back to the times of Lemuria or Atlantis; people were no different. The only difference back then is to infer individual humans had the more magical ability at their fingertips. The need for more and more in those times would involve more and more magical powers, to take over, annihilate oppositions or to become as powerful as God himself. It is using the power afforded to them, which caused the demise of Lemuria and Atlantis. As their audacity and lack of integrity led to the Highest God, punishing all who lived. Now some did receive forwarning this was about to happen. A few of the most impeccable servants left and went to Egypt, Peru, India, etc, taking many of the scrolls and tools with them. The remainder, however, met their demise, by way of a cataclysmic earthquake and ensuing flood. Wiping and sinking these islands off the face of the Earth, sending them to the depths of the oceans.

The Creators experiment was concluded and what came from this was a much less evolved *Homo sapien*, who spread throughout the Ancient world and developed at a much slower pace than previously known. However, even with these species of a less evolved human, among them were those who beheld such knowledge and power, using this to create still incredible wonders of the known world today.

Yet, what about these experiments in human existences. How could we improve ourselves? Especially when today, many people hold the Atlantis code or complex in their karmic records. One, which informs their soul from deep, of an ensuing cataclysmic doom that could befall humankind once more. After all, what have we learned from those previous lifetimes? Anything? Maybe not, because when you explore human greed and its blatant disregard for caretaking the Earth which sustains our very life. You can easily envisage it all happening again. What do we have to learn? I believe we need to learn how to surrender to the awesomeness of the Creator and the more magnificent beings who live in higher dimensions. If this too becomes too fictitious, then perhaps we should start small. Begin with reverence, love, trust, and then we could move forward to connecting our sacredness once more to Divine belief and reverence of s/he who gave us life afterlife. For example, maybe we could begin with honouring our ancestors and those who walked this Earth before us. Instead of holding onto blame and disquiet of how they lived and impacted on us. Because then we realise we are connected to their stories through our DNA. Instead of judging, maybe we offer forgiveness instead.

Chapter 8
Working with Nature and Her Aspects

We have journeyed through the elements of Creation, now let us explore how the dynamics of nature, influence who we are, and how we begin a sacred journey back into the graces of these elements.

The natural elements of Earth, Air, Water and Fire are the building blocks of our survival. The Ancients knew how to work with them via an act of appeasement and reverence. They knew full well their survival depended on this relationship being nurtured. Each one of these elements gives and takes life, yet in the western world, we have moved to a place of blind belligerence in considering the importance of this. Our belligerence comes in the form of inadequate relationship; we have placed our humanness as being the primary importance over sustaining our survival. We have become locked in a super-hero complex of growing incomprehensibly invincible. So we think! Until the power of nature, shows us the contrary, with unprecedented floods, fires and weather changes. Even our air quality is under hijack, though this is more likely due to human tampering than natures displeasure with us.

However, we view the four elements, and we are guilty of becoming complacent in our lack of knowledge in appreciating how lifeless we would be without them.

Perhaps our complacency is born out of a lack of reverence for the intelligence residing in these elements. Our Ancient ancestors knew this and understood it's importance as the basis of one's survival. Not only did they celebrate the spirit living within the elements, but they also observed the spirit in all inanimate things too. They knew life exists as a living thing, not merely in the obvious of humankind, animals, insects, plant life, herbs and vegetation. But also in the mountains, the rivers and everything else made from the elements.

Consequently, the problem with modern-day life is down to our lack of respect and acknowledgement of nature; we do not even consider the importance of working with nature for our survival. This is down to our inflated, egotistical importance in human life, where we have assumed a super-hero complex. Until of course, we are faced with the immense power these elements create, as shown in earthquakes, raging fires, storms and flooding, it is then we realise just how inconsequential we are. Yet, the first thing we do when faced with such disasters is to seek someone to blame for the catastrophe and inconvenience natures force caused us.

Our Ancestors knew the importance of this relationship, but not as equal to, but instead as in the symbiotic connection, a child has to its Mother or Father. Our Ancestors knew how to respect, and their belief was to show reverence by first asking permission to drink the water and to plant their crops in the soil of the Mother. They also knew about the importance of asking forgiveness, especially when they did something wrong or disrespectful, or if they were negligent in practice. Even when faced with disasters, they turned first to appease by creating offerings to the Deity symbolised in the element.

It is for us just as crucial as modern-day humans, whether we are following a spiritual path or not. To understand the wisdom in building a relationship, with all the elements. Whether it is Pachamama, Mother Earth or Gaia, or Father Sun, our life-giving fire. The Air we breathe, Mama Wayra the wind who carries the air, to the life-sustaining water known as Mama Cocha without which there would not be any life on this planet. The only way we can have a relationship is to deepen our inner gratitude, love and praise for the spirits of the elements.

Perhaps first, we should understand the importance and meaning of the term relationship.

Relationship means having a connection to something other than the material. Knowing how the relationship between two things is and how they are connected. As in a symbiotic relationship,

A symbiotic relationship means a mutually interdependent relationship. Two different kinds of organisms live together for their mutual benefit and survival.

A more philosophical type of relationship begins and ends with ourselves. It isn't found in the influence of a figurehead such as a Priest or Vicar who steps in to do the work for us. Neither is it located in a 'how-to' set of instructions, wherein we only read a script or book which informs us how to have a relationship.

The act of building one comes in the form of a more rooted connection via the act of doing, by honouring and placating. We can only achieve this by immersing ourselves in nature and then learning how to imbue them into our being. To do this, we begin by venerating the guardians, by conversing with each of the Mothers, Orishas, or Deities of air, earth, water and fire. This type of ceremonial work shows us how to feel the connection throughout every cell and organ of our bodies. Then as we imbue this inside, we understand not only the significance of being one of the same, but how natures elements are a vital component for sustaining our planet. A sad fact of western culture and even for many of the indigenous cultures which have evolved into modern-day living is in our lack of reverence. It waned throughout the arrival of all patriarchal religions, due to handing over the reins of our personal, ecclesiastical responsibility to religious figureheads. In doing so, we lost our sacred connection to Divinity and the consorts of Mother Natures Elements,..

While this is the case we have become disconnected from the importance of doing ceremonial work and with this, I feel concerned Mother Nature, will take matters into her own hands, to show us how insignificant we really are to the sustainability of this planet. Unless we learn to reconnect and to help restore balance, especially now as we see how the world has become terribly out of balance. Therefore it is the duty of every one of us to restore a relationship and harmony here on Earth after all this is the real mission of a superhero. Before it is too late.

Rebuilding a Relationship to the Elements

Before you do these nature visualisations, make sure you will not be disturbed, for 15 mins or so. In setting the scene, gather all the items listed below before you begin

You may even like to tape the blessings beforehand and add some music.

Work with one element per week or longer if desired. To build a deeper connection and to be able to imbue the aspect by working physically with it thoroughly.

Each journey or meditation should begin first by taking slow breaths. Breathing in for the count of four, hold for four and release for four. Repeat for around seven sets.

Water Mama Cocha

You will need a bowl of water, with some beautiful blue flower petals sprinkled inside the container. And a pretty cloth.

The petals will reflect the beauty of the water and its fluidity.

Place the bowl of water in front of you, on top of the pretty cloth.

Consecrate the water by holding your hand's palms facing down into the water and say out loud.

Blessing for Mama Cocha

Through the law of love and the through law of grace
Bless this water with gratitude, love and praise.

I ask permission to connect more deeply with the Spirit of Mama Cocha.

(You can add the names of Olokun, Yemoja, Mami Wata, Danu, or any other Water God you have a relationship with).

I offer forgiveness if I have been disrespectful or disconnected or neglectful in any way.

I am grateful for the teachings and lessons Mama Cocha *(or add the name of your chosen Water Deity)* will offer me.

This water is now consecrated, may the blessings be.

Meditation Journey

Get comfortable and begin your 4-way breathing.

Read aloud or tape this visualisation journey.

As you breathe slowly in and out, Tune into the infinite consciousness of your entire being. Feel its present in your feet, your legs. your hips, diaphragm, heart centre, neck and your head. Sense the power of awakened consciousness inside your head. Experience now the power and connection to the Higher worlds. Envisaging a light that shines brightly in between your pineal gland and third eye. This is the light of wisdom, and it emits its vibrancy like a beacon throughough the whole of your being.

Now, imagine you are in a garden, and it is the most beautiful garden you have ever seen. Everything in the garden reflects its beautiful aliveiness, with shining sparkles and brilliance. The colours seem to stand out emmitting shades and hues of colour you have never seen before, as every accent or particle of this place exudes vitality.

You are approached by a line of women who are elegantly and ceremonially dressed. They come towards you carrying large palm tree fronds. These women are Iyami, the Ancient Ancestral Divine Mothers, and they are here to honour you today.

Some of these women step forward, and help you lie down on the lush, vibrant earth. It feels warm, soft and welcoming beneath your body. You immediately feel a sense of peace and safety as the Earth holds the weight of your body on top of her own body.

A Mother steps forward and places the most beautiful and stunning effervescent opal discs along all of your frontal chakras. Each opal disc is imbued by your energy centres, you feel your chakras open, like a flower in bloom as you welcome these effervescent articles.

Softly a gentle hand urges you to turn over.

A Divine Mother then places several obsidian discs inside the chakras running down your spine. As each obsidian disc is placed on your back, you begin to feel secure and protected.

These discs are to activate your bodies internal medicine.

You are urged to turn onto your back.

Another Divine Mother steps forward to place laurel leaves around your head, and she drapes strings of red, black, gold and silver beads around your neck, she then puts a silver symbol of an owl over the top of the beads. The owl symbol as all bird symbols are a sign Iyami are near.

They help you to stand up, and they lead you to a lake, a Mother informs you that this is the home of Mami Wata. Gently you are guided into the coolness of the water, you are mesmerised by the beautiful colours of azure and green, and you witness the water suddenly begining to feel alive and energetic around your body. Two of Iyami hold your shoulders and gently submerge you into the depths of the cool, calming waters, as your sink down you can feel tiny fish swim all around you.

As you feel the water all around your body, you are reminded of the beauty of Mama Cocha and how she provides sustenance, essential for your life and the lives of every living being on this planet.

You are really enjoying this connection. So, stay as long as you like.

When you are ready, arise from out of the water.

A Mother steps forward and wraps you in a beautiful silky soft blue robe. For the first time in a long while, you feel cared about and coveted.

You feel an intense gratitude to them for showing you how to connect to the Earths precious life affirming waters.

After what seems like several minutes.

You find yourself back in the beautiful garden once more. Use your breath to connect with your inner divine self. As you breathe in and out, you arrive back inside your room.

As you come back into the room, place your hands inside the bowl of water.

Infuse the water with your innermost expression of Gratitude, Love and Praise for Mama Cocha and the Divine Mothers Iyami.

Now gently using your hands, anoint yourself with this ceremonial water, on your head, back of the neck, throat, heart, solar plexus, base, hands and feet.

Keep this bowl of water for one week to remind you to connect with Mama Cocha every day, by anointing yourself with her fluidity. As you do, remember to hold an innermost expression of gratitude, love and praise for her.

During this week, go and visit other bodies of water. Lakes, the ocean, rivers, streams, waterfalls, and even the puddles after it has rained. Or go and stand out and let the rain cleanse your body. Drink as much pure water as possible to wash and take in Mama Cochas essence inside the whole of your body. Remembering to use the blessing at the beginning to enliven its medicinal qualities.

When the week has finished, take any remaining water and throw it outside your front door. Towards the West Direction.

Earth Pachamama

You will need a large bowl of fresh earth and a pretty cloth.

Place the container of earth from the garden (do not use bought compost etc) in front of you, on top of the cloth.

Consecrate the earth by holding your hand's palms facing down over the soil and say out loud.

Blessing for Pachamama

Through the law of love and through the law of grace

Bless this earth with gratitude, love and praise.

I ask permission to connect more deeply with the Spirit of Pachamama.

(Add here other names for Earth Goddesses if you wish, like Gaia, Mother Earth etc.)

I offer forgiveness if I have been disrespectful or disconnected or neglectful in any way.

I am grateful for the teachings and lessons Pachamama will offer me.

This Earth is now consecrated, may the blessings be.

Visualisation Journey

Get comfortable and begin your 4-way breathing.

Read aloud the visualisation journey or pre-record.

As you breathe slowly in and out.Tune into the infinite consciousness of your entire being. Feel its present in your feet, your legs. your hips, diaphragm, heart centre, neck and your head. Sense of the power of consciousness inside your head. Experience now the power and connection to the Higher worlds. Envisaging a light that shines brightly in between your pineal gland and third eye. This is the light of wisdom, and it emits its vibrancy like a beacon throughough the whole of your being.

Continue to allow yourself to inhale and exhale at a natural pace.

With your eyes closed, allow the patterns of light and shade to relax you and sink slowly into them until you start to envisage yourself arriving at a place that seems like heaven. A place that feels very surreal in both frequency, image and colour.

Everything seems to stands out in 3D. The shapes and colours of this place are unlike anything you have seen on Earth before.

You begin to notice men and women all dressed in different styles and colours. Notice the brightness of their dress, some are wearing all yellow, some wearing all blue, some wearing all red, and so on. Even the men seem different, and they look seem stronger, yet like peaceful warriors.

One warrior is carrying iron objects, and another who seems to be both male and female at the same time, without showing any distinction to either sex and yet is dressed as neither, he is immersed in looking after his herbs and vegetation. There is so much going on here, and you find it challenging to take it all in.

The place you find yourself in is the sacred home of the Gods and Goddesses.

Again Iyami comes to greet you, and you notice one is holding a sizeable pot-bellied pot full of jewels and crystals. Another is holding a box made from wood containing coal, another comes forward holding a bowl of silver. Another carries items made from tin and copper, and lastly another has brought a large box of salt. They lay the pot-bellied pots and other vessels all around your feet.

They gently beckon to you to lie down, and your body feels the softness of the grass beneath it. As you lie there, someone covers the whole of your body with a white chalk. Suddenly your body begins to sink into the earth. You panic a little until one of The Divine Motghers

Iyami places a hand on your shoulder and whispers in your ear, "Trust, all will be well."

As you allow your body to sink through the fertile soil, through the bedrock and the stones of the earth. You find yourself in an underground cavern. As you catch your breath, your eyes become accustomed to the darkness. You look around and notice the glorious riches, that Sweet Mother Pachamama, Mother Earth holds within her belly. Jewels, Diamonds, Silver, Gold, Copper, Tin, and Salt. As you observe these riches, you begin to understand the abundance inside Pachamama and how she provides everything her children need.

You are enjoying this beautiful and deep connection. Take your time, spend as long as you like here.

You will know when it is time to leave and come back.

You arrive back to the heavenly space you were in before.

As you breathe in and out, you return to your room.

As you arrive back into your room, place your hands into the bowl of earth.

Infusing the Earth with your innermost expression of Gratitude, Love and Praise for Pachamama.

Keep the bowl containing the Earth for one week so you can reconnect with Pachamama every day, by placing your hands deep into her belly. As you do, remember to hold an innermost expression of gratitude, love and praise for her.

During this week, go and visit Pachamamas bounty, by visiting gardens, Caves, forests, the beach, remember to lie down on the earth whenever you can, or walk barefoot outside. Visit vegetable markets or flower stalls to take in the richness of everything she provides. Eat a wholesome and plant-based diet for the week. Try and buy as much organic food as possible to appreciate the absence or need for any chemicals which poison her body and your own body.

When the week has finished, take the bowl of earth and throw it, in the direction of North.

Air Mama Wayra (or Oya)

You will need, an empty glass bowl, a pretty cloth and some incense.

Place the empty container in front of you, and light some incense.

Consecrate the Air by holding your hand's palms facing down over the empty bowl and say out loud.

Blessing for Mama Wayra (or Oya)

Through the law of love and through the law of grace

Bless this air with gratitude, love and praise.

I ask permission to connect more deeply with the Spirit of Mama Wayra.

(Remember you can add the name of your own chosen deities of air).

I offer forgiveness if I have been disrespectful or disconnected or neglectful in any way.

I am grateful for the teachings and lessons Mama Wayra will offer me.

This Air is now consecrated, may the blessings be.

Visualisation Journey

Get comfortable and begin your 4-way breathing.

Read aloud the vision journey or meditation

As you breathe slowly in and out, Tune into the infinite consciousness of your entire being. Feel its present in your feet, your legs. your hips, diaphragm, heart centre, neck and your head. Sense of the power of consciousness inside your head. Experience now the power and connection to the Higher worlds. Envisaging a light that shines brightly in between your pineal gland and third eye. This is the light of wisdom, and it emits its vibrancy like a beacon through the whole of your being.

As you continue, allow, your breath to breathe at its own pace.

Visualise yourself on top of a high mountain. At first, you find it hard to catch your breath because of its height and altitude.

Take in the glorious scenery of the other mountains you see in the distance, and you can almost touch the clouds they feel so close. As you look down at the clothes you are wearing, you see you are dressed from head to toe in silver. As you marvel at the shining silver of your outfit, you notice Iyami; Divine Ancient Ancestral Mothers approach you.

One of the Mothers walks forward, and you see she is carrying a pot-bellied pot. She urges you to look inside the container.

You see a white swirling mass of an indescribable substance. You look curiously at the Mother, and she says, "This is your Ashe, the purest energy you were born with."

As the wind begins to increase, you can feel the breath of Mama Wayra wrap herself, all around you.

Then, The Divine Mother Iyami asks you to stand in the shape of the Vitruvian Man, with arms held aloft at right angles and legs mirroring the stance. As you do this, a lightning bolt comes from out of the clouds, and it strikes you.

After this, you do not remember what happened. When you finally awaken to find your silver attire has been replaced with white clothing.

Suddenly you hear a tremendous rumbling as the mountain begins to open up beneath you. You fall and find yourself inside the mountain.

You land softly without hurting yourself. Once inside you notice an inner shrine. Again you are approached by one of the Divine Mothers Iyami, and she asks you what gift you would like to receive? She offers come guidance and says it must be one which will help you to feel more connected and which will instil a better relationship between you and your spiritual nature.

The Mothers step forward with three pot-bellied pots. One has silver inside, the other has gold inside, and the third contains your purest energy, 'Ashe'. You can take something from whichever pot you feel you need.

The Silver pot contains the energy to right all the injustices you feel you have had in your life.

The Gold pot contains the essence of abundance and blessings.

The third pot contains pure energy, which will infuse you.

After you make your choice, you find yourself outside and on top of the mountain once again.

The wind wraps her delicious self around the whole of your body. As she does, she whispers into your ear, her voice is so light it fills the entirety of your being as she says, "You are protected so hold the Ashe of existence inside you."

Enjoy the connection, take as long as you need.

Suddenly it all finishes. You find yourself back in your room once more.

As you return to your room, place your hands into your bowl of Air.

Deepen the Air with an innermost expression of Gratitude, Love and Praise for Mama Wayra or Oya.

Keep the bowl containing the Air for one week as you reconnect with Mama Wayra every day, by placing your hands deep into her existence and Ashe. As you do, remember to hold an innermost expression of gratitude, love and praise for her.

During this week, go to visit Mama Wayra's high places of power, by visiting high sites, mountains, hills, open spaces, or the beach, breath deeply when you come to these areas. Enjoy the outdoors as much as possible this week, walk, run, play and always as you do breathe deeply of Mama Wayra's essence. Feel the joy of being able to breathe deeply from her.

Light natural incenses and take note of how the smoke swirls and flows away from its source. It creates impressive shapes. Now go and open a window and bring the fresh air into your home.

When the week has finished, take the bowl of air and throw it, in the direction of East.

You have nearly completed imbuing your Spiritual DNA activation with the Elements.

Fire Inti Tata

You will need a pretty large candle and a beautiful red cloth and some matches.

Place the beautiful candle in a fire-bowl in front of you, on top of the red fabric.

Consecrate the Candle by holding your hand's palms facing down over the candle (unlit) and say out loud.

Blessing for Inti Tata

Through the law of love and through the law of grace

Bless this fire with gratitude, love and praise.

I ask permission to connect more deeply with the Spirit of Inti Tata.

(Remember you can add in your own chosen Fire Deities names here)

I offer forgiveness if I have been disrespectful or disconnected or neglectful in any way.

I am grateful for the teachings and lessons Inti Tata will offer me.

This Fire is now consecrated, may the blessings be.

Visualisation Journey

Get comfortable and begin your 4-way breathing.

Read aloud the visualisation or pre-record

As you breathe slowly in and out. Tune into the infinite consciousness of your entire being. Feel its present in your feet, your legs. your hips, diaphragm, heart centre, neck and your head. Sense the power of consciousness inside your head. Experience now the power and connection to the Higher worlds. Envisaging a light that shines brightly in between your pineal gland and third eye. This is the light of wisdom, and it emits its vibrancy like a beacon throughough the whole of your being.

.

As you continue to inhale and exhale at your bodies natural pace.

Envisage standing before a gigantic mountain. There is vegetation all around, trees, plants and you can see a waterfall cascading down the mountainside.

As you stand there take all of the sights in.

You suddenly notice a vast doorway appears on the face of the mountain which slowly opens up. With such a roar and the sound of stone scrapping on stone, it opens to reveal a portal for which you are required to enter inside, and with trepidation, you walk inside.

Once inside the mountain, you begin to descend, as you do you finally find you have landed on a plateau, as you look around, you notice that this is not merely a mountain, but you are deep inside a volcano. The Divine Mothers Iyami approach, but this time you notice there is a male present. You sense this is going to be a ceremony. As the Mothers approach, they cover the whole of your body with a substance that seems like volcanic ash. As you look down at your body, you notice your ashen body is also covered with a red robe.

Suddenly the male steps forward he is holding a cockerel. With widened eyes, you watch in shock as the man throws the cockerel into the volcano's raging lava.

As the cockerel descends, you think the cockerel will surely die. Until all of a sudden, the flames of the volcanoes fire turn blue.

The Divine Mothers Iyami and the male ask you to jump into the blue flames.

You, of course, hesitate, yet still, you jump in. Instead of the flames burning and engulfing you. You notice how the blue flames tickle around your body.

You see the cockerel, and you are amazed it is okay, you reach out and grab hold of the cockerel.

Both you and the cockerel are evacuated from the fire, unscathed. When you come away from the mouth of the volcano, you look down and notice you are now dressed head to toe in white robes. As you emerge, you are given a gift of a gold ring with a black stone. This ring symbolises something extraordinary. And it's teaching is shared with you here.

"Out of complete devastation, something new always finds its way. New life always emerges from the death or destruction even when the event seems to be of colossal proportion. Life still finds its way, as each death and rebirth offers a unique chance, to do better. Mother Nature is never destroyed; she always creates a new way to reform life once again. Nature can generate existence from what seems to be an impossible foundation. Life can burst forth out of a piece of toxic land and will explode from the smallest crack found in a concrete jungle. Yet life needs the fire, it requires the water, and it requires the air all working together to manifest its essence and substance. All it asks is for you as a member of humankind to work symbiotically with its elements and with gratitude, love and praise in your being."

Take as long as you like to ponder on these teachings.

Suddenly it all finishes. You find yourself back in your room once more.

As you return to your room, waft your hands through the candle heat. Of course be mindful not to burn your hands.

Imbue the Fire with an innermost expression of Gratitude, Love and Praise for Inti Tata.

For one week, light the candle every day and as you reconnect with Inti Tata, by placing your hands through its essence. As you do, remember to hold an innermost expression of gratitude, love and praise for her.

During this week, understand the importance of fire, as an element that can create new form even as it destroys, and how it can transmute from one material to another. From the heat, it provides, to the light it gives. Understand how the fire was integral to the survival of our ancestors and the great feats of engineering it has produced.

When the week has finished, take the candle and bury it in the earth, in the direction of South.

You have now completed imbuing your Spiritual DNA with the Elements.

Congratulations!

Chapter 9

The Ancestral Gene Pool

I must admit before I fully understood my extraordinary lineage and what it meant to the spiritual path I was already following and in service to, I viewed any ancestor work, differently. As a Shaman, I worked with honouring those who went before, my ancestry, though not at a level which I later learned to be sufficient. I can share a much more explicit description of this by sharing my experience.

Our Seer, who is herself a Sibyl, suggested to me I should obtain a divination from a Mami Wata Priestess, to better determine how I could be in service to Iyami, as I move forward in my relationship with them. She had been shown the learning I needed right now, and for this to manifest, I would need to experience a consultation with this Mami Wata Priestess. To discover how any further training and attaining of a pure-at oneness with spirit and the Divine Feminine could further help me along this path. I made an appointment with the Priestess who resided in America. I eagerly awaited the time, and I anxiously rechecked the time differences to ensure I would be ready to receive the divination. It turned out, after sending a picture of myself and my date, and place of birth along with the question, already detailed by the Seer, the divination had already taken place. When Mama rang me precisely at our pre-planned time, she relayed the findings of the prophecy quickly and earnestly, after a quick resume of the path leading me to her.

As I rushed to take down the notes, I became puzzled at her conclusion.

Mama began, "You have some misfortune and betrayal in your ancestry," she shared.

"I have?" I replied, shocked.

"But I have dealt with my ancestry already," I replied haughtily in the way, only an indignant English person can respond.

"Yes, you do, and unless it is cleared you will not be free," she shared.

Questions, ran through my head, like how who and when? "Can you tell me where it came from?" I asked.

"No," she said. "However, you can come and have a ceremony here with me, it will involve a sacrifice of an animal, and then you will need to take a bath, and I shall have to give you a ring."

All I could say was, "Thank you, Mama," wherein she became animated and excited to talk about Ireland, where I now reside. As I thanked her, I said goodbye and sat with the information she had shared with me.

I admit I was perplexed as I could not think where any misfortune and betrayal would hail from within my family line. I spoke to my mother, who was at this stage in her late 80s. She couldn't recall where it could come from either. Then a warning arrived which unveiled, a clue wherein I should not look towards where it was likely, but rather where to me felt unlikely. The possible route for me would have involved tracing back through my maternal bloodline. Merely, because this is the bloodline where my lineage connection is to Iyami. Therefore I decided to trace my father's line, and As my father had already passed in 1992, it was a complete shot in the dark. The only clue I had was in reviewing some of the information I did have, this hinged on the fact my grandfather (on my fathers' side) died in a misfortunate accident while working at the docks in Newport South Wales.

I began the obligatory and sometimes confusing foray into the genealogy sites. I started to build up a sketchy picture, but still, it wasn't offering me the complete answer. At this point and a loss, I went back to the Seer and asked for help. I shared the divination, and I had received from the Mami Wata Priestess, explaining, for me as a western woman, the idea of the sacrifice of any animal was outrageous even to consider. She then offered to do a further divination on my behalf. In doing this, she would get a much better idea of how to help me progress.

It is in the divination and this is how it was revealed to me.

"In the first part of your Divination, The Mothers (Iyami) explain how you have spent many lifetimes as a Priest /Priestess of Earth, Sea and Wind, in the ORISHA/IFA Tradition, The HATHOR-Sirian Alchemy Tradition of Old Egypt, and as a Student of Imhotep the Healer. Within these, you excelled. In this lifetime, you are to embody the element of Fire. It will be aided by representing your lineage.
You Are A Priestess/Child (100 per cent) of the NANA BURUKU (Called Nana BUKKEN-in the west). She is in a central part of the Pantheon of the Iyami, and she contains an active element of (Earth/Air/Water. All the Mami Wata elements). She is the Mother of all Orishas (who are the deities), and Her Priesthood is Matrilineal!. Therefore you should first clear your Ancestral Line, by seeking out help from The IFA FOUNDATION (This foundation is overseen by the Iyami in Africa and will connect and begin your journey of accessing the Divine Tools necessary. This Destiny will lead you to Nana Bukkens Sacred Mound which connects Earth and Sky in the Etheric Africa/World."

I know as you read this, and it is how I felt when receiving the divination. I thought I had become part of 'Mission Impossible'. As I embarked on attaining a further piece to the puzzle and hopefully more clues as in discovering the misfortune and betrayal in my ancestry. Naturally, I contacted the IFA Foundation and relayed my story to a remarkable lady. Who listened intently, and she too became excited as we shared our stories. I underwent some teachings with her. Whereby during one of the lessons, she shared with me the importance of Ancestral worship and appeasement. As I followed the required ceremonies, Having first viewed them with a western worldview. I felt disconnected and a little disingenuous in my approach and dedication. When it was time for the next round of ceremonies, I decided to ditch the western head and embody my ornate spiritual self.

Well, what a difference, as I diligently checked in with my ancestors, I received the connection I desired. For me, the information became active during my dream state. As I received messages from an Aunt, my Fathers sister. She showed me first their childhood home, amongst the terraced streets of Newport, though in showing me this, I was shown a shadow hiding in the corner of the house. The house appeared in the dream from a much older time-period, not as I remembered it as a child. The vision showed the house stocked with older furniture and a blackened fire grate, in essence, possibly Victorian.

As the connection began to deepen with my ancestors, I began to develop the genealogy analysis. In doing so, I discovered a lady whom I didn't know, had already compiled a family tree on the masculine side of my Fathers line. This lady lived in Australia, so I contacted her as soon as I could. I received a lovely email back from her. Indeed she was a relative and turned out to be a second cousin.

She also forwarded two in-depth family trees. As I read through them, my newly acquainted second cousin, became intrigued to know why I needed the information. I relayed as much of the story I could, (without scaring her off completely) When she said to me, "Do you know it's funny a lot of the men along the male line had kidney problems?" Well, a light-bulb lit up in my head as my own Father also had kidney problems. Having had an operation to have one removed before he passed. Having shared this with her, she proceeded to tell me more.

Back in Victorian times, one of my Fathers ancestors enjoyed a good life, living with his beloved wife and children. One day his beloved wife became sick and sadly died, leaving him alone to care for his two children. In those days, this was quite a feat for any man who was both breadwinner and Father. After some time passed, he met a new lady, who was herself a widower with children. They got married, and his new wife and her children moved into his home. Fast forward to later on when my relative was in his late 50s, he too became ill, with kidney problems and he died due to this. Leaving his second wife, her children and his children. Now, what transpired after this, provided the answer. Having died his house automatically was left to his new wife. And when further on down the line, she also became ill and eventually died. And this is where the misfortune begins because when the will was read. It discovered how the second wife, had written all her step-children out of the will and left their fathers home to her own children. Leaving his children without any claim or compensation.

This evidence was further confirmed by a dream I had wherein the ancestor came to me, along with his two children, again they were presented in the scene in the old Victorian view of my Fathers home. The ancestor arrived looking very pitiful and sorrowful, as he held onto his children. He said, "Forgive me, I didn't know what else to do, I needed a Mother for my children, and I married her."

This eureka moment was followed by gratitude for how the magical processes in discovering the truth were unveiled to me. All through the process of Ancestral worship and appeasement. I finally understood how and why it is so important to be able to work with our ancestors. Even though it is widespread for the Vodun and latter Santeria/ Voodoo derivatives of African religion to do so. As well as some of the other cultures around the world, such as South America, China and Japan and other Asian cultures. To elaborate further, is to understand better how important this practice is and what it means?

I feel in the West, we mainly hold the fact that when our loved ones die and pass over, they are no more. In truth, the focal point for most is the cemetery, which is attended and maintained. Yet, even though many people who lost their family members go and chat away to their loved ones at the side of the grave, they often seem to accept the deceased are indeed dead and are no more. Though for other cultures and the African religions especially, this is far from the case.

The Ancestors Are Alive

There is sometimes a misconception brought about by belief and influence, concerning what happens when we die. Do we go to heaven and spend the rest of our time, basking in the glory of the Creator. Or, maybe we join our loved ones and remain, blissfully spending time there. Or do we become locked in a limbo of denseness, flailing around in the lower dimension? Few of us know the actual answer or route of passage a physical body takes when we pass from one state to another state on death. Many however have experienced out of body experiences, though we have yet to reconcile where these experiences take place. The reason for saying this is when we cross through the borderland between this life and the next realm, there are many sub-dimensions within the fourth dimension, where we go while in our spirit body. For me, I have yet, to discover the correct route our spirit takes to determine the death state recapitulation, rest, reward and whether we are required to take physical form once more, or evolve to a higher state.

Some rules of thought explore, the great journey of death from the physical state to the spirit state. One which then undertakes a journey through the desert lands of the abyss. Where they are met along the way, by loved ones and Angels who help with a recapitulative view of the route their lives took. Looking to see how the events and situations propelled us towards accumulating karmic debt to the right actions taken in service to collect the good karmic reward, therefore cancelling out the debt and replacing it with karmic credit. If we are lucky, then we can be weighed by the scales of justice, to see how our karmic tally has been.

After we finish our life assessment, we are led to the water's edge, where we drink of the 'waters of forgetfulness' and make our way further across the lake to rest and recuperation, awaiting our next incarnation.

The Ancestors

Whatever form, death may take, it is immaterial when understanding the importance of our ancestors. Because the truth is, our ancestors, are integral to our wellbeing while we are here in life. It is also common within the Western Culture, that our way of remembering them is to tar them with their human behaviours.

Now another misconception is built around a suspicion wherein those ancestors, even while dead, still embrace the same human behavioural personality they exhibited when they were in physical life. It isn't the case. Why? Because of the amount of time they spend in recapitulation and life review when they pass over. As we take time reviewing the life we have left, to understand what happened, how we influenced others, how we lived, where we were useful or on the other hand, what harmful deeds we did. As well as seeing the situations where we were in service to humanity in some way. There is a lot to sift through and even though the Christian form of judgement day, isn't quite the case. We still review our past life with the help of an angel guide. Remember how life was lived, determines Karmic debt or Karmic reward. It is then accountable for the type of incarnation, offered next time around. When we finish here and enter the realm of the otherworld, remembering there is an absence of time measurement in this environment, we probably arrive at the kingdom of our ancestors. From here we can serve, guide and aide our living kin.

Let me add a caveat and a clause, regarding those who when living, were evil and had little or any respect for human life, other than to watch it continually suffer at their hands. These are the ones who will not take an opportunity for a life review, where their karmic debt can be reviewed. Of course, some souls who are inherently shadow beings do have little or no interest in evolving. These end up in another area of the underworld, and yes they can still incarnate back into life and into situations, ready to create mayhem on some miserable unsuspecting human life. It comes in the knowledge of, where there is light and dark, there are those fifty-plus shades in between. Where there is a heaven or many heavens for different beings, the same can be said of the many types of hell (a Christian concept I know), but it still paints a symbolic picture of reference.

When our ancestors enter the ancestral environment, they may still retain some memories of the life previously lived, these memories are more like ethereal recordings. Yet, they do not maintain the bitterness, sadness or even their misguided behaviours. They can and do feel sorrow or regret, depending on what they did. In some cases these ancestors when they die, hang around their family members, because they feel so much shame and regret, for what *they did.* These are the discarnate spirits, those who for one reason or another become trapped betwixt the spaces, left to wander due to unresolved issues. These spirits or ghosts are the ones who need specialised help in moving home.

Therefore for those in living form, it is imperative to honour and keep this ancestor environment sweet and honoured. After all, who wouldn't want their army, dedicated to ensuring good fortune and wellbeing?

Merely from personal experience, I honour the knowledge of understanding how our current family members lives interact with those of the past. Especially when we look at common illnesses or addictive behaviours, to even the similarity in the events, misfortunes or successes. All of these, repeating and replaying generation after generation. With this in mind, the importance of asking for help from the Ancestral space would clear so much karmic debts, running through individuals and their bloodlines.

Ancestral Worship and Appeasement

In the west hold a somewhat egotistical view about the process of appeasing. Somehow it bruises our egos and hurts our inflated selves, the mere notion we should 'doff our cap' or 'bend our knee' to anything living or dead is abhorent for some people Yet the real meaning of appeasement isn't in the same vein. I view this more as a way of showing gratitude and offering something to infuse wellbeing by keeping my ancestors on my side.

Honouring the lives they lived, acknowledges and offers thanks to them, for giving us life. However, their lives were, is an indication of the era in which they lived, and the circumstances offered to them at the time. Choices and free will all come into play as they do in our own lives. Do you really want to be persecuted or judged because you made a wrong decision, by your own family or peers? Of course not, because there are mitigating circumstances for all parts of our lives. None of us can judge another, without first walking a mile in their footsteps. There is no blame to be placed on those who fall prey to addictions, or steer themselves down a path of crime or violence, without first understanding why?

Similarly, the child who is sexually abused and lives a life of dread and fear and who grows up to become the bully or abuser themselves. Towards whom and where we point a finger of accusation in the first place, becomes the basis of contention. Everything has a source a beginning, where something happened for the very first time. How it repeats and manifests down the gene pool, is nothing more than like attracting like. However, by saying this, everyone has a chance to stop and cease the effect of all the causes. Therein lies the ability to learn and evolve, away from the initial mistake or even the manifestations of the gene pool.

Such is the reason for living, as each turn we make is a chance to right the many wrongs.

There is, of course, an overriding fact and this is, without our ancestor's sacrifices, and sometimes a lifetime of suffering, we wouldn't even be here, to judge and criticise.

The Ancestral Altar

To begin the process of reconnecting with your Ancestors is quite simple. All you need is a small space, either inside or outside. A space dedicated purely to your ancestors. Perhaps you can build a shrine or even better, make space on a shelf or a table, either is suitable.

First of all, find the space, you would like to dedicate to your ancestors.

Clean it well, with water and salt.

Place a cloth or a specific textile to denote the space if it is inside the house.

If outside, build a small weatherproof shelf or altar plinth, you could even use a slab of stone, or denote an area by placing rocks or crystals, to create a boundary.

Within your dedicated space, add items like photographs (only of deceased relatives) and objects belonging to those who passed over, for example, your grandfather's pipe or your grandmother's diary. Add crystals representing a specific relative, like rose quartz for a beloved aunt or mother or even different earth stones. You decide how you would like to symbolise your ancestral group or an individual ancestor.

Make space for candles or even a lantern (if outside).

Add other sacred items if you wish, like religious artefacts or feathers etc.

You will also need to ensure space is left for small plates of food offerings and alcohol or tobacco.

Get a small glass bowl to ensure the ancestors always have access to clean, refreshing water.

Congratulations you have created a special ancestor space!

How to Appease the Ancestors

Now you have your dedicated space, you can begin the process of adding offerings.

In this case, the offering can be comprised of their favourite food items, or you could offer a small portion of any meal you cook. You could even add bread and cheese if you wish. Be mindful, that any food left longer than 24 hours will need to be cleaned away. Also, people question, why doesn't the food-stuff disappear? Try and understand, it is purely the essence of the food items which is imbued by those in the next environment.

Get a small glass like a shot glass to add their favourite alcoholic beverage.

Put clean, freshwater into the transparent glass bowl.

When you have added these items, you are ready to begin the connection to your ancestors.

The Ancestor Worship

The process can be done in a couple of ways. You decide the way forward for yourself.

Either a daily check-in or have a weekly, or once a month meet, or have a specific day every week dedicated to your ancestral connection.

Before you begin, light a candle and ensure all offerings are placed on your dedicated space.

Add fresh flowers or the petals of flowers if you would like.

You can either open space around you by saying a prayer similar to this:

Say the Prayer Aloud

Winds of the South, Keepers of the South Great Serpent, Wrap your coils of light around us.

Winds of the West, Keepers of the West, Mother Jaguar, Protect this Ancestral place.

Winds of the North, Keepers of the North, Hummingbird, Ancestors, Ancient Ones.

Winds of the East, Keepers of the East, Eagle Condor, Connect us to the holy Mountains.

Mother Earth, we have gathered for the healing of all your children.

Father Sun Grandmother Moon, the Star Nations, Great Spirit you who are known by a thousand names, be with us here and guide us.

Ah, Hoh.

Or if you wish to use this Ancestor Prayer, which is my preference.

Note: Include only those who have passed over.

Speak the Prayer out Loud

I offer blessings to all of my departed bloodlines

I honour all those whose blood and cells are within me.

I respect all of you who came before me.

I offer special blessings and gratitude to:

My Father......... (Father's Name) .... speak it x3 times (Only if passed over)

(If you know the names include them in the relative space and call them all three times)

My Paternal Grandfather .... (Grandfather's Name) ....

My Paternal Grandmother ...... (Grandmother's Name) ......

My Paternal Great Grandmother.

My Paternal Great Grandfather

My Mother...... (Mother's Name) .... Speak it x3 times (only if passed over)

My Maternal Grandfather ...... (Grandfather's Name)

My Maternal Grandmother

My Maternal Great-Grandmother

My Maternal Great-Grandfather

I include love and gratitude to all those whose names I do not know, yet your blood and cells are part of me.

I offer the coolness of this water so that you may be calm and comfortable.

I offer this food and drink from my table to yours.

Please accept the light and energy, so you have brightness and strength.

Even though we live in separate spaces,

I sense your presence here on Earth and take strength and wisdom from your continued support and guidance.

May your guidance help open the paths and roads and the paths and trails of those I love.

May you offer strength and courage and give good health to me and those I love.

May your wisdom bring harmony, balance and prosperity into my home.

I am honoured to be guided and protected through the spirit of my Ancestors.

I am genuinely grateful for the gifts I receive from you and the support you offer.

The roots of our family tree of life, extend outwards a long way.

I am honoured to cherish our relationship.

I await the messages from beyond the veil.

Guide me to interpret these messages wisely.

I honour the sphere of Our family Pachamama

Through praise, to you all.

Ashe Ashe Ashe

When you have said your choice of prayer, set a timer on your clock or phone, for 13 minutes only.

Then once this is done.

Sit within the space, and here you can either talk about your day or ask questions or even complain if you feel it is appropriate to a specific Ancestor. This time is entirely personal and to be used for whatever reason, you would like to connect, sometimes we need help, sometimes we yearn to talk to a loved one, other times we merely require answers. There isn't a measured outcome or protocol from what is already set out in this chapter.

When the 13 minutes are finished, say your goodbyes or your 'I love yous'.

Then wait for more messages to come in your dreams or even in your waking life.

The best results come from regular check-ins.

Enjoy this process as it reveals to us the magic of keeping the lines clear as well as receiving a sense of peace, where we realise there is no death, only a continuum of life force, a connection that will never end. But one is merely separated by the thinness of veils or perhaps knowledge in knowing the only thing that has changed is how the spirit moves from one place to a different environment, and it is a space where each has contact with the other.

There will be so many gifts and even a sense of justice to be accessed from doing this Ancestral work.

Chapter 10

Dark Energy

The content of this chapter is a heavy one to write and to explain, especially as it is not my intention to induce fear. Yet this subject for many is rarely spoken about, let alone reach someone's consciousness unless influenced by a horror film or creepy show. However, I can easily express my opinion, and it is demonstrated in the work I do as a Shaman. The ability to harm someone using sorcery, hex or even toxic thought is exceptionally viable. I wrote about the way a person's behaviours, actions and vocabulary can and does affect others in my book, 'Living Shamanism, Unveiling the Mystery'. Though now, when I look at the content, I included back then merely provides the groundwork for this chapter. As I am now confident, there is much more available for people to use these means as they are readily obtainable and easily accessible, the internet being one source. The intent required by a potential saboteur, witch or even a Voodoo Priest can be received as an influencing power to any unsuspecting victim.

Considering this, I know any individual who practises Black magic or hexing uses a different kind of creed and is entirely the opposite of the type of practice, for example, white magic. I conclude this fact based solely on the idea, Black Magic tends to hurt individuals, so much so via inducing serious illness to even death in some cases.

The term Black or White magic is explained as:

Black magic seeks to abuse someone's will, via influence or manipulation. It is done via using spells, potions or even dark spirits.

White Magic is a skill used to gain medicine from herbs, plants, crystals and other corresponding items and using a higher vibration to aid someone in moving forward in a healed state. However, there is a further tier in the form of High Magic, and it works as a system based on the Divine support using the Infinites pure intent to correct any distortions in emotions or to right and balance distortions on a larger scale.

An illustration of the differences can be further explained by defining the variances. Sometimes Magicians or Shamans or indeed anyone working in the esoteric fields, claim to be of the light. Yet their actions and intentions are of the opposite. They seem to say one thing and act with their feet firmly placed in the underworld. These people are known by the term 'dusk' practitioners. Which as it intends, is someone who can swing between both light and dark. This type of practitioner is often dangerous and can easily do a lot of damage either in healing or via a sorcerous intent.

What Is Sorcery?

To describe sorcery in the simplest of terms, let us revisit childhood fairy stories or even the scary movies we watch: tales of wicked witches turning their subjects into rats, Horror films showcasing demons who possess people. The stereotypical view of sorcery is something that exists outside of us; an evil and dark circumstance created by a supernatural being, who comes from a dark dungeon, and hails from a mythical land. Yet it is these very stories that embody the substance and legacy of things that happened a long time ago. We can find an idea of the truth of what happened, before the onset of the written and published word. Yet we hold the view based around our western concepts, these stories are merely made up and are non-existent?

However, witchcraft and magic when ushered by magicians is more common and close to home than we may think. There are lodges and covens all over the world, who meet in secret on certain sabbats, to either celebrate or to do some magical work. This work is not always for the benefit of humanity, on the contrary, it is sometimes done to take the energy or to inflict sorcery on a victim.

Then, of course, there is the sorcery we individually inflict on another, perhaps a friend or colleague who has hurt us, even though we may not use spells and potions to obtain the power to destroy. As I mentioned earlier, the sorcery found in thought, proffered by the mind is just as powerful, as are words.

The question we need to ask is, 'Do we remember any instances where we may have used thought transference, as a means to hurt others'?

No? Well, consider this, to be guilty of using sorcery whether knowingly or unknowingly is as simple as thinking or saying something negative about someone else. Gossiping and complaining about others has become a natural way of life, throw-away comments ushered by thoughts and even when told in the heat of the moment while venting to a friend, or obsessed over in the quiet of your home. In terms of energy work, is classed as sorcery.

Taking this one step further towards the dark side, to attempt to control another person's thoughts or freedom is another example of sorcery, whether this is done intentionally or not. Manipulation or control over another human or animal, even if undertaken light-heartedly, still affects their energy. If you utilise a method of power in any of the following ways, it can be perceived as sorcery:

- Controlling yourself or others
- Being out of control
- Using power as a form of manipulation

What Is a Dark or Shadow Energy?

There are several categories of dark energy to be aware of, and the first and simplest is the darkness we hold within ourselves, better known as the 'shadow' or suppressed self. The second is a type of darkness that comes from another being or entity:

'An entity is a being that doesn't possess human life as we know it. Something that exists by itself: something that is separate from other things'

Having an inclination to dark energy or even being the host to an entity can also provide the ability to create a shadow, one which can act semi-independently from its host. The difference is this: some shadow beings or entity's do have enough power to feed off their host's inner harmful desires and feelings and project them out into an unsuspecting world. Other shadows, known as parasitical entities, can attach themselves to a life force and use the essence of their host to sustain itself. It can also influence its host via gaining control of his/her mind, and it is often shown in an unsuspecting host, who suddenly changes his/her behaviours or actions, even to the point of suddenly adopting an addictive nature, wherein one which wasn't there before.

The Shadow Within

Additionally, we can now further an understanding of the shadow within. Known as our intangible Self; the unseen part of our nature that hides in its hidden recesses until the switch goes on, wherein it unfetters itself and is unleashed. Our inner shadow is brought into the light via the mirrored aspects offered by those who enter our lives. Sometimes it is the angry, frustrated, hurt part of self that comes forth when we are forced to defend ourselves. You might find yourself justifying questionable actions with coherent, logical arguments as to why you were right, and the other person is wrong. Or, there is a deep and inner need to acquire justice, fuelled by a lingering urge for resolution.

Each one of us possesses a hurt, spiteful child who bursts from the bowels of our being to attack others when threatened. Every one of us can resonate with being at times judgemental, biased, prejudiced and opinionated, and for me never more so, than when engaged in watching reality TV programmes! The self-righteous inner self will air its views and when sated, withdraws back to the shadows until it is allowed out of its box the next time. If we explore negative thoughts in more detail, we might argue how a person can become the very thing they choose to believe in (if that belief is hungry enough). Better explained as thoughts create opinions and opinions can create personalities.

The Outer Darkness

We know, energy comes in many forms. There is the selfless, beautiful and natural energy derived from Source and Nature: which is created by the purest of, natural essences. Imagine a scale or spectrum of colour from white to black, It is unrefined natural energy I talk about and it is located at the farthest end of the white part of the range. Its opposite is a dark, power created by an emotionless, unfeeling being at the other end of the scale. Humans, themselves can create through negative thoughts and actions, anything in-between the range, in fact throughout the many shades of grey, to even having the ability to stretch via action alone, outwards towards the extreme edges to the black end of the spectrum.

This form of energy varies anywhere from the lightest of greys to the blackest of blacks. A final example of dark energy has a considerably more dense, low vibration. This energy is deemed by religious institutions as 'evil' or 'demonic'. A power, despite its personification, doesn't possess an ill-intentioned agenda, emotion or feeling. It is merely a lower vibrational entity located over at the lowest end of the black side of the spectrum. Hijacked and utilised by Black Magic procurers or Black Witchcraft practitioners. The human-made religions have termed or even 'demonised' (forgive the pun), this being many times in the Bible and inside its sermons. Used as a way to push parishioners into understanding their actions or get them to give up their sinful natures.

What does the word 'demon' really mean?

The word 'demon' derives from an early Greek term meaning 'a wise guardian spirit'.

Now doesn't this definition sound a long way off the Western interpretation of the word? Today's use of the word 'demon' has significantly altered its meaning since the Ancient Greeks first used the word.

There is a broader correlation we must explore, to fully appreciate the legacy these entities termed as demonic, or evil have. One we must do without the hysteria and fear abasing tales thrust upon us by old myths and religious institutions. Generally, demons are seen to be non-human and to exhibit malicious existence. (Though, I could argue the point regarding the knowledge based on how some humans are extremely capable of generating enough negativity to sour their psyche into a miserable and degenerative state). Everyone battles with their inner demons, whether forged from negative and challenging life experiences or spending long periods alone and immersed in harmful and destructive thought processes. Some of these are powerful enough (over time) to alter anyone's reality.

If dark energy does not originate from a human, then we often mislabel demons as being destructive, angry, lost, disembodied ghosts or spirits.

Spirits or Ghosts can become trapped and lost in emotional and mental purgatory. These entities are a once residual imprint of human life, who lived in physical form and for various reasons did not ascend towards the 'light', or I should say did not go through the afterlife process. They exist in a world without form and are unaware of their own sense of being non-physical here on Earth, but lost betwixt the worlds. These spirits have, in fact, not moved forward to the next environment, choosing to stay connected to the living. Why? Perhaps because of unresolved issues, or guilt or because they need help to move forward. The latter occurs most commonly after experiencing a quick death, through accident or operation, whereby they do not sufficiently understand they are dead!

Over the centuries, hundreds of ghost stories have been shared. Though, it is important not to ridicule those who have been physically affected by terrifying or unearthly experiences, experienced, by what they believe are ghosts or dark energy. Yes, spirits utilise many ways to get the attention of the living; ranging from positive to negative. It depends very much on how they lived their life when in physical form, and whether they were ready or conscious about moving over to the spirit realm. However, there is an unknown fact, regarding those who believe ghosts can act destructively, these types of Spirit activity are often known as poltergeists. You may be surprised to read how; poltergeists are not commonly ghosts who, scratch or throw things across the room. They are not the ones who push you down the stairs or sit on your chest either. You may be shocked when I reveal how the purveyors of such actions are indeed the Faery kingdom! Yes, I know, it's a shock, right?

This shock comes from how we, as a race, disregard the otherworldly beings who exist alongside us. Not only do we deny them, but we have also placed their existence into the legacies of fairy stories and the legends found in books. We have been seduced into a belief. Fairies are tiny little beings who are dressed in brightly coloured dresses, designed in the shape of leaves and flowers. Who flit and fly using their shiny little wings around the flowers. Sorry, as I may well burst your bubble here, but fairies are often around 2ft, sometimes taller, who scamper about the land and they have little patience for human beings at all. They are the ones who get extremely agitated if humans, build or change things. Their fury is often felt when we kill animals or insects. They are also forced to action by an arrogant male who has complete disregard for what he does on the land or to the home, and they are further agitated by mental instability too.

So the next time, you experience a bump or scratch or feel something shout at you, first ask yourself, have I disrespected the home or land? Did I hack away and tear down a bush or tree in the garden? Or did I unnecessarily kill a spider or something else? Did I change the footprint of the home and build an extension? If you are a victim of Faery displeasure, I suggest you learn the lesson, and the next time you want to change something, ask their permission first. Leave an offering of milk, cake or honeyed water outside, before you bumble headlong into tearing or killing something. Then you may not possibly feel their wrath.

Energy and Entity

Before we further explore what a demon is? We should first understand the power and force our energy has within its physical form, and we can then observe how the same energy gathers strength and momentum once we leave the physical plane. As we know, energy is never destroyed. It merely changes form. Why would we think as soon as we leave the physical world this energy necessarily goes away? We should also explore a sensical idea, regarding different kinds of beings who co-exist around us, not only understand how this is possible but disregard our narrow thought constraints, which infer there is only human, animal and mineral.

There is animate life in everything, a tree is living, and the same breath is imbued into the wooden table in your kitchen. The food we eat, whether animal or vegetable was living and that life enters into our bodies when we eat it. The mountain or Hill you visit, is teeming

151

with life, not only the insects, flowers and fauna growing on top of it. But also the hill itself, is a being of the land. It has its consciousness, as does every animal, bird and insect. The cosmos is alive and full of different consciousness's, as is the inner Earth, rivers and oceans too. Anything can exist, in differing forms and densities, there is life everywhere, whether we see it or we do not, These many different beings, live, without caring if we believe or not, they do not need our approval to co-exists either. They are here, irrespective of our existence. Though they do require our attention and respect when we walk over them or take from them. They can and will show their annoyance if we do not ask permission to enter a sacred grove or walk boldly into an ancient holy site. They can also punish if they see fit, especially if we have indulged our arrogant human ways, there will always be a price to pay.

Understanding Demons

However, I believe there is a more plausible way of understanding demons. To do this, we should first explore the two sides of the white and black scale, I spoke about earlier. Moving forward from this is to explain duality. So, What is duality?

'Duality is an essential concept that must be grasped if one wants to have a deeper understanding of life. ... Duality teaches us that every aspect of life is created from a balanced interaction of opposite and competing forces.'

The opposite and competing forces of the same thing, where there is light, there must be dark. It is an analogy used earlier in the book. We cannot have just one, as there must be a polarised opposite in everything. When the Creator created energy, it was formed from out of the vast nothingness, for example, from out of the void, came light or life. Yet, while this happened, both light and the void remained.

Throughout the evolutions and manifestations, different forces of nature and deities came forth. Super Gods and Goddesses, Angels and Archangels, Star Beings, as well as the first five root races of human beings. Yet, what remains within all is duality an opposing force.

As humans evolved and were influenced by the latter human-made religious practices and proclamations and laws. Humans were relegated from being able to commune with Deity under his own volition, until religious figureheads took over regular man's ability and duty to talk directly. Inflicting hierarchy as a way to attain power, therefore ensuring the holy men, gained responsibility for all spiritual practice. It created a shift in power as well as a separation, allowing influence, great wealth and social standing stayed held within the religious systems.

How this was maintained, was during the sabbath sermons and through the religious laws and taxes imposed on the common man. The weekly Sermons required a common man to live in servitude and obedience to the country's chosen spiritual practice. And to ensure compliance, they spoke about the fear of the dark powers, expressed and espoused during the weekly Sermons and through the religious systems, moral laws. People became afraid of anything dark or evil, and they were already brainwashed into believing they were the products of sin, having been expelled from the Garden of Eden, due to Eves, disregard for the Almighty's laws. It became the downfall of women, as she became secondary to men, even her husband or Father.

When someone acted irreverently or was seen to be possessed, the Church, deemed this as being owned by a Demon or Devil, the church were the only ones with the power and processes to be able to remove the entity. Therefore, establishing more control in the form of being mans, moral saviours.

However, it is clear many people back in history and still, today, do not fully understand who Demons are. They only have the church's view on them, which is still today questionable.

I have researched the view of the Hebrew texts while looking to define the term Demon. Otherwise, most of our information, regarding what a demon is, comes from the Abrahamic Religions viewpoint.

Despite[12] the translations, there is no word in Hebrew equivalent to the English word 'demon', nor any word that communicates the same meaning that the term describes in English as an evil being in the service of the devil out to destroy humans. That idea today has been shaped by the imagination of medieval writers and popularised in the modern church in terms of evil beings against which Christians need to wage 'spiritual warfare'. Yet, the ancient Israelites lived in a world in which that view of 'demons' was not part of their culture or way of thinking.

There are four other parallel terms and phrases that are used with the word translated as 'demons':

Strange or Foreign gods, Abhorrent Things, Demons, Gods and New Ones.

It seems evident in this context from these parallel terms that the term translated 'demons' also refers to the gods of the surrounding peoples that posed a threat to Israel's worship of Yahweh. In this passage in Deuteronomy, the broader context is an appeal, in the form of recounting Israel's failure to worship God and their practice of worshipping the idols of Canaan, to worship God properly as the only God.

It leads to the conclusion that the word translated as 'demons' does not refer to anything close to what we moderns think of as demons, but is a pejorative term to refer to the idols of Baal worship that are declared to be nothing at all (compare Isa 44:6-20, What is emphasised is that they are 'no god'.

---

[12] http://www.crivoice.org/demonsot.html

Considering the research in both the terminology and legitimacy of description, detailing what a demon is, could now be better explained via the context of both duality and how words are misused over time. There is also the added element of using manipulation of a term when applied to inflict fear or to create obedience. Perhaps we should view the idea of a 'Demon', as an opposing force, which doesn't have an emotional agenda at its core. But instead a type of Deity who is destructive without the tendency to be malevolent. Instead, it is a being without evil tendency, yet its force and existence is necessary as part of the Creators bigger plan.

Utilising Energy to Cause Harm

I remember when I first began my journey along the spiritual road. I studied Paganism and also Green Witchcraft before I fell headlong into the world of Shamanism. I wanted to find the innate meaning of life, beyond the physical, and to find a more natural form of belief and practice. I was searching for profound, authentic expression, away from the dogma and ritual form of all the patriarchal religions. I felt I was looking for something away from the constraints of society, yet something more accessible for my heart to attune. One of the very first rules I remember learning was; 'Harm none'. It became a mainstay to my new beliefs and practices and even when challenged by hurt sent from the court of others. I never misused energy as a way of retaliation. Even now Fourteen years later, and with a newly found research into my lineage, I am somewhat shocked or should I say worried about how common it is to employ the services of a Black Magic practitioner or Witch.

Furthermore, there is a much thinner veil between the light and dark spectrums nowadays. Then again, there is quite an ensuing and blatant fight going on between duality, regarding the light and the dark armies going on now too. When they say 'times, they are changing', this is worryingly true. As I mention the fight, I see it both in real terms, as in the way corruption is transparent in many walks of life, as well in non-reality terms.

I am unsure whether it is because there is a lot of unhappy people out there with so much poverty and hardship abound. And because humanity is actively desperate to dig themselves out of what seems like a living purgatory, to find a better life. So much so, the energy people use in wishing for their desires to come true, plays straight into the hands of the shadow. Add to this a feeling of vulnerability and addictions, all of which adds more weight to an already toxic soup of rancid negativity. One which the darkness feeds on and utilises at its whim.

History has superseded itself, after hundreds of years of slavery and servitude, all of which exists in Western cultures too. The gap between the have and have-nots, remains and as long as it exists, nothing will change for the common man and woman. The latter is unfulfilled and feels immense pressure, and daily living is a round of continually paying out money, mainly to the governments and the influencers. People's resources are stretched beyond safe limitations, and this creates depressed citizens. It is in a small way, how I, as a human, can understand the desperate need to carve a better life for their family.

However, the effect of using sorcery or black magic does create distortions in the fabric of the Earth's plane and not only this, but it can also develop tears within its finite structure. As well as creating an imbalance within the harmony of our world. Furthermore, we should also consider the morality of those who practice this. Because they are soldiers of darkness, working solely in the court of their masters, openly working to create as much disorder, chaos and distortions here on Earth. These parasites are responsible and add to an already unstable world and bringing it closer to home, they are responsible for creating much more misfortune in the lives of others.

In some cases, they are guilty of vampirism, as they prey on the weaknesses of those who buy their services. Somewhere down the road, a line is crossed, and energy is manipulated and stolen, this, of course, creates the imbalance and breaks the law of the Universe. Which will be explained in the next chapter.

Soul Bandits

If you do not know what a 'Soul Bandit' is, then perhaps you remember the film 'Single White Female'. It is a film about a girl who lives on her own and needs a housemate to share the rent. A seemingly wonderful girl turns up, and during the interview, everything indicates to the homeowner, she would make a great housemate. As the film plays out, worrying things begin to happen to set off alarm bells, as the housemate isn't all she seems. What transpires, becomes the stuff of nightmares, as the housemate, becomes obsessed with the house owner and wants to become her.

Soul Bandits come in many shapes and guises and can be female, gender-fluid or male. They arrive in your life amidst a flurry of flattery or out of curiosity. What often begins as an open, fast and flowing friendship, where there is nothing they won't do for you and in offering you support is a common ruse of friendship. Of which can turn in a relatively short amount of time towards, jealousy and envy. There is a saying, and it holds relevance within this chapter: 'Familiarity breeds contempt'. Whatever the source circumstance of meeting a soul bandit, there is seldom little clues as to their true intentions. A soul bandit wants nothing other than to be you! Or to destroy you! It is the purpose and his/her/they end game. The emissions of a soul bandit in its active and mythical form are one of the intended vampirism. Even in this state, wherein an energy vampire, drains the lifeforce, a soul bandit has a darker and more pervasive edge. As it wants to take over not only your soul but the life your soul has carved out for itself.

How Does This Work?

Well, it begins as I said in admiration or friendship. Then the more familiarity between you both. The more the tide starts to turn, the soul bandit watches everything you do and say, and they perceive your lifestyle or ability through the eyes of their conscious state. The spectrum of danger ranges from mimicry to obsession, and there in the middle of these two lies jealousy. They say 'time will tell', and there is truth in this, how the relationship moves forward, depends on how well you begin to notice the energy of a soul bandit.

What Are the Telltale Signs?

The first one comes in how they observe you, as I said, they watch how you deal with and how you react in different circumstances. The response from a soul bandit will be to observe your vulnerabilities. Once these have been revealed, he/she/they will then use them as they grow in strength and begin to challenge, in doing so they either start to question your feelings or reactions, or they uninvitedly give free advice and propose similarities towards themself. On the surface, this seems mundane and non-invasive until, in some extreme cases, the energy becomes darker and nastier. Soon their admiration is replaced as their ego takes command and distorts what they perceive. When this happens, jealousy and envy begin to take over. It is here, the energetic strands of sorcery begin to take over, as their energy cords are focussed on either sabotaging you or on invading your space. On the level of physicality, this person starts to put you down or gossip about you to other people. On the level of the mental, their actions and behaviours create insecurities within your mind as you are placed in a position and are required to explain or defend yourself. Again when we have to over-explain ourselves, we walk headlong into the territory a soul bandit knows very well. The battle ensues, where a war of words is bandied back and forth, and whoever has command over articulation wins, or forces the other to submit out of mental exhaustion. Usually, it is the soul bandit who wins because this is how they energetically steal your lifeforce, it is the arena they know very well.

With the ever pervading realms of social media and email, the soul bandit is stronger and more pervasive than usual. Within these mediums, courage and boldness replaces the fear of confrontation and shyness. As the ego grows in stature and creates its world of roles and personalities, all fuelled by an inherent lack. There is inside us all a repressed, bully or in some cases, repressed violent tendencies.

Soul bandits have one Achilles heel, and it is usually found in the wounds they carry. Difficult and challenging lives often, create these wounds, as they look for an outlet to distract themselves away from these. Distraction turns to ensure others feel the same desolation and hurt they feel inside themselves. The bandit needs to take your joy, your light and turn it into darkness. Jealousy and envy turn into an avenging and pursuing energy attack, call it sorcery or term it black magic, whatever its name, it is dangerous!

Soul Bandits have an active power to destroy and to challenge everything you have and hold, and this energy becomes a spell, a hex or a curse. One which will require to be cleansed from you. Either by ceremony or in a cleansing bath.

If you are a victim of a soul bandit, I advise you to seek the services of a trusted professional if you require this type of work.

Chapter 11
Understanding the Basics of Protection

When we talk about protection, it isn't merely about how we can protect ourselves from being harmed physically or mentally. Or is it solely about ensuring we protect ourselves, our loved ones or our homes from a physical or violent attack? Acknowledging the need for protection is better defined here as a means of safeguarding our energy or auric bodies from paranormal or psychic attack, we are just as likely to be susceptible to an attack from the unseen realms as much as we are in the physical world. Especially now as there is much more dark intent wholly transparent in both realms. As said in the previous chapter, life is often challenging, and the gulf between the have and have-nots is apparent to all. The TV and social media, parade the lives of the rich and famous in front of us daily, this causes low self-esteem and lack in our poverty consciousness. All in all, within a lot of the population, this lack can cause jealousy and envy, and a drain on precious life force.

Now I am not suggesting to you to go around looking over your shoulders or to try a new technique of sleeping with one eye open! Knowledge is power and safeguarding your vital energy source is a way of sustaining yourself from being affected by sorcery or malicious intent.

It is a fact. We live in a time where we are much more likely to become exposed to both social media attack and cyberbullying. We are vulnerable to those who gain power and justice when typing a malicious text/post or email. Finding ourselves victims to the envy of another's jealousy or long-held resentment is commonplace. The inability to forgive is also a treacherous road to go down, ensnaring both the victim and perpetrator in a pattern of hostility, a negative patterning which quite literally becomes an energetic life sentence for both people involved. As the saying goes, with an added clause,

"Hell, hath no fury, like a woman or man scorned."

It, in part, is true, and it is right to say many people can hold onto how they were wounded or hurt for many years, even a whole lifetime.

In other parts of the world, sorcery and malicious intent when focussed on another are taken very seriously. It is well known that in extreme circumstances, individual members of society (who are known purveyors of magic whether they are a Magician, Witch or Shaman) can curse a victim, in return for money. In some African countries, these purveyors are treated with suspicion. It can be deemed as an extremely potent magic, often sent by way of a curse, hex or spell. Belief in something this strong can carry very active energy when sent to an unsuspecting victim.

Whatever we have encountered in life, knowingly or otherwise, can and will have power over us. Whether it is a power that comes from our own source or externally, the power of the mind as a source of malicious provocation, can be very damaging when directed towards a person.

Now there is more need for both protection techniques and maintenance of the energy body than ever before. Life as we know it can be purposeful and giving, or it can become an endless round of emotional and psychological events and experiences. The latter is, of course, the only way we learn our soul lessons, as we undergo the many tests and initiations spread throughout our path. What happens to most of us is our resolve becomes weakened when we are faced with an emotional challenge. Challenges create conundrums and frustrations, and we automatically resort to using up our mental or emotional energy to find a solution to recover from the event.

We can view our vital resources as pots of energy, which are spread out among life's needs.

Vital Life Force (Ashe) and Sami

When we are born, we come in with a life force. In the Orisha Yoruba tradition, it is called Ashe, which is the vital life force blown into a human being by God it is also called the Divine Breath, and it is a spiritual power that we can use to create anything. In the Qero Tradition of the High Andes, it is an infusing of energy and it is known as Sami, refined natural energy which brings pure light energy into our aura.

Our vital Ashe is a flow of energy which can work in the present, backwards and forwards. As it creates anything, it is responsible for all aspects of our life, emotional, physical, relationships, work and our spiritual journey. This vital Ashe is a resource pot, and it is spread between our survival, (home, resource, food and clothing), Family unit, Friends and health. We can quickly squander our vital resources due to the decisions we make in our day to day life. And we can also have it stolen from us, by others. When our vital energy system is susceptible and weakened, whether this is from a combination of lifestyle choices or an energetic attack, the different pots of vital resource, become an ever-increasing round of energy share out. For example, if we made a lifestyle choice to drink ten vodkas every night and eat a selection of fast food. Then our physical body resource pot and our health pot becomes depleted. Add to this an attack of jealousy or envy, then more resource is taken, and we begin to get depleted. Unless our Ashe is topped up, by making wholesome repair choices, then eventually we begin to negate our precious resources. Hence our physical or mental health begins to suffer, leading to survival issues etc.

Let Me Share a Personal Story with You

At the beginning of 2015, our family endured some health challenges. The prognosis from the medical end was favourable, and the health problems were all curable. Yet on the emotional front, they created a highly emotive and challenging aspect in the way our feeling body dealt with them. I guess it was the adage around fear of loss that was behind all emotions, let alone the challenge and strength needed to support our loved ones as they went through these challenges. As you can imagine, each of us became utterly wrapped up in the process of care and support. During this time, I knew I was physically and emotionally drained. While I took time away from seeing clients, I chose to continue maintaining care for clients who needed support via email or text. It was during this time, I contracted the winter flu and was laid up in bed for a week.

Suddenly out of the blue, a client of mine who was undergoing life challenges, sent me a somewhat toxic email, describing my current lack of care for their current challenging situations. Even though the email derailed me during my own vulnerable time, I replied and extended my support. I explained briefly in the email how we were undergoing some very personal health issues within our family unit. Only to be met with a further unbridled attack. Due to my emotional vulnerability, the energy directed from the person, via email, was malicious and robust. So much so, it swept throughout my energy body and into the home, causing a lot of havoc and chaos, when I recovered from the illness and the attack, the home and myself needed protection and energy clearing. I have shared this story with you to express how easy it is to become a victim of an energy attack when in a vulnerable state.

At that time, many of my vital resource energy pots were being drained of energy. From the emotional pot, the family pot, the health pot and the spiritual pot.

Some Valuable Protection Techniques

Shamans are well versed in creating protection around the energy body and home. They have the necessary expertise in clearing spaces, including, the house, land and workspace. Cleansing negativity and dense energies, using a variety of techniques, visualisations and ceremonial rituals.

However, there is still a great deal; you can do to keep your own family and home safe.

Remember this simple rule If you are fearful or hold onto the belief whereby, sorcery, spells and magic can create untold harm, then, of course, anything sent your way with malicious intent will affect you! Remember fear is the downfall of us all and if we let it in, then we open the door to all manner of infiltrations. The very thing we believe in can come true, not because of the powerful way it has been sent to you, but because of the way you think it to be so. Don't forget as much as the mind can be a powerful ally, and it can also be a damaging enemy too.

How to Protect Your Home

Boundary Protections

This simple method will involve a little effort. This method is suitable if you believe someone is targeting you or your home maliciously. Using salt creates a boundary line and will disperse negative influence when it is directed towards the house and its occupants.

You will need:

A large bag of salt

The amount of salt required is dependent on the size of your land, house and boundary. If you live on acres, you need only be concerned with the perimeter of your home and immediate vicinity. Of course, you are welcome to do the whole of your property, though it may be better to make a mixture of salt and water in a bucket or add it to a spray bottle and spray the boundaries of your fields.

Example:

For the house and immediate vicinity. Sprinkle dry salt around the edge of your boundary, make sure you create a salt line, nothing can cross. Then place the salt in a line across all entrances to the home, for example, the front and back doors. **Please note**: the salt is sprinkled outdoors. Also, if you experience heavy rainfall, then you may need to repeat the salt-line until you feel the energy has subsided. It is safe to say; only when you are sure negative energy can no longer get through, this weakens the sender's ability.

Containment of Malicious Intent

This method is suitable if you feel that someone is maliciously focussing negativity or ill-intent towards you, the home or its occupants.

You will need to do this short visualisation every day (or night) for a couple of weeks until the energetic message has been received by the perpetrating party. I think it is more powerful when done at night-time, as in many cases, this is when most instances of malicious intent are sent. If you know the person who is inflicting this towards you and where they live, then this method is beneficial. If you do not know their home, then you will need a stronger sense of visualisation to imagine them in a home.

Please remember that this isn't something that will harm them.

The Visualisation

Take a few deep breaths slowly in and out, settle your breathing down to a good rhythm

Close your eyes

Picture the person at their home. Imagine them inside the house.

Now visualise a large thick wall of ice building up around their home.

Make sure you visualise the wall of ice covering every part of the home of the person in question. It should be thick enough (around 4ft thick) to surround all the sides of the house, left and right, all around the back and front of the house, as well as above and below the house so that sorcery cannot leak through towards you. You must ensure the wall is thick and there are not any gaps showing in the ice.

'I Don't Mean You Any Harm'...

This next process is done, to ensure you do not want any unwelcome or uninvited energies on your land or in your home. By speaking aloud this intent, you will ward off any stray or inquisitive notions sent by another or whether the energy comes from the unseen realms. This process is perfectly adequate when dealing with minor energetic attacks.

You will need to do this at the front and back doors.

Stand firm in a powerful stance, at your front door while holding one arm out in front of you, in a 'stop do not cross' manner.

State this out aloud

"I do not mean you any harm, but you are not welcome here, you may not cross any of the boundaries of my home or land." Repeat at the back door.

Removing Dense Influence from Your Home

Sometimes you might unwittingly invite someone into your home who has left a residue of harmful intent. It may be someone who caused an argument or verbally attacked you in your own home. This process also works well if you suspect someone has directed sorcery towards the home and you feel it is inside the house. There are sure signs that this has occurred:

Symptoms

- There are more than a usual number of rows occurring between family members.
- Things in the house keep breaking.
- Fuses or light bulbs keep blowing.
- Objects seem to jump out of your hands.
- Family members are prone to more sickness than usual.
- Your pets seem to be on edge or may not want to go into some rooms.
- The drains block or keep on blocking.
- You have problems with the water systems in your home.

You Will Need:

Either some Californian white sage in leaf or smudge wand form or a Palo Incense Stick (a naturally impregnated wood from a tree in the Amazon)

A candle and matches

A fireproof bowl

Method

Light the candle and place it in the fireproof container.

Pick a place to start, either at the front entrance or in a particular room.

Remember that wherever you start, continue to walk around in a clockwise motion.

Light the chosen herb, either Californian sage or Palo Santo stick (Please Note: the Palo Santo takes a while to light when it catches fire, and the fire goes out, use the smoke to smudge the room).

Walk around each room and using your hand in an anti-clockwise circling motion, as if you were unwinding something. By doing this, you are unravelling the influence from the area; you are clearing.

Repeat this process in all areas and rooms of your home for maximum effect.

Protecting a Family Member While Travelling

This is an excellent method when used to safeguard someone while they are off on their travels.

It is a visualisation method to be done the night before they go off on their journey.

Visualisation

Visualise the family member standing in front of you.

Now draw around them in a clockwise motion, golden tendrils of golden bands of light. Bringing these bands around the whole of their body from head to toe.

Remember to include any of their travelling companions too, as well as any modes of transport they will use, such as the car, train or aeroplane.

Then, when you have drawn the golden bands around the traveller (and if needed the travelling companions) imagine your loved one with bare arms and legs.

Now, imagine you are holding a power stone or protective crystal.

Blow into the stone or crystal with the intention of protection while travelling.

Next, draw the crystal or stone in a downwards motion against their bare arms and legs.

Note: You can also carry out this process in person with your loved one present if you wish.

Protecting Yourself: Generally or While Out and About

As we've mentioned, it's essential to keep yourself protected in day to day life. It will help to ensure you don't pick up any negative entities, or even moods from other people. Remember, when we are vulnerable, and our emotional or psychological states are low, this is when we are most likely to be influenced by energy from the physical or unseen worlds.

A note about the unseen influence

As briefly spoken about earlier, there are other realms as well as our physical material realm. These are separated only by a differing vibrational frequency. The difference in these frequencies can be compared to the octaves on a keyboard. The higher the note or octave, the more refined the energy contained within. Therefore, if the realm is linked to a lower octave or frequency, it is most likely these unseen entities residing here are denser in form. In their fight to survive, they sometimes (only sometimes) attach themselves to those here on the physical earth. These lower density realms should not be confused with the religious depiction of 'hell'. Energies of a lower frequency should not be termed as 'bad or evil; It is merely different from ours. If you look at a pool of water and the water is cloudy or muddy, this doesn't mean the water is terrible, it is just water. The same applies to lower frequency energy.

As a species, we should not even presume we are the only types of living energy in existence!

General Protection Methods:

Process 1: Smudging the Body

To clear and protect yourself instantly, you will need:

Californian white sage
A fireproof bowl
Matches
A candle

Method

This method is similar to smudging your home.

Light the candle and the sage, then using the sage smoke, waft it around your body to clear your aura.

Remember to smoke the front, back and sides of your body, paying particular attention to the areas under your arms, your legs and feet.

Process 2: Instant Protection

Find somewhere to sit quietly; wherever you are. It could be your car, a crowded shopping mall or even at work, and You could also find a toilet.

You are going to place a protective veil around yourself.

Place your hands in a prayer position over your heart centre.

Now, lift your arms above your head (towards the area above your crown chakra).

Then, as if you were fanning open a golden veil pull it down from this area and cover your whole body with golden light. (The process is akin to a peacock opening its tail feathers).

Remember to cover your back and front areas as well as the sides of your body. You are aiming for the action, similar to placing yourself within a golden shell.

Protecting a Car and Its Occupants

Process 1: Crystal Bag for Vehicle Protection

You Will Need:

A small drawstringed bag, big enough to contain your crystals

Do this either at the Full Moon or in Full Sunlight

You will need to source a piece of Fluorite, Clear Quartz and Black Tourmaline

Make sure you cleanse your crystals after purchasing them, either by leaving them out overnight in a dish in the bright moonlight or out all day in a bowl in the sunlight.

Charge them for the purpose by holding all three in your right hand (or, the hand you write with, this is your power hand) Blow into them three times while visualising saying these words, "I charge you to protect my car and its occupants every-time I/we travel in it." Place the crystals in the bag and place them somewhere safe inside the car.

Process 2: The Protective Symbol

You will need to decide what your preferred symbol of protection should be.

For some, it could be a cross, a crystal, an element like fire or water, a pentagram, or even some other symbol that means something specific to you.

Visualisation

The night or morning before you are due to take a trip

Visualise the car.

Then visually place your chosen symbol over the top of the vehicle. The symbol will create a protective state over the entire car and its occupants.

Chapter 12

The Significance of Cause and Effect

We are the architects of our reality! Everything happens not in isolation but as a direct result of something else already set in place, **a cause**. To bewilder you, even more, this cause could have also stemmed from a past life and has become lodged as karmic debt.

(Your soul records all events and their effects from previous lifetimes, especially when the origin, has not been weighed, measured and balanced within a system of good deeds, versus negative actions, when we refer to a karmic debt – it is a reward system of credit and debit. Similar to the Ma'at system from the old kingdom of Egypt. Ma'at: Is the Ancient Egyptian Goddess of Truth, Justice and Morality, who decided when a person was ready to enter the afterlife. By weighing their soul against a feather. She represents the concept of balance and order in both heaven and earth.)

To further elaborate the karmic theory, there is always a chance for us to resolve unattended causes and effects, so we do not become overburdened in a constant debt scenario. These are fortuitously fed into our consciousness in both waking and during our dream states. Creating perfect opportunities for you to correct the imbalances, via a continuum of repeat occurrences, to ensure the origin has a chance to be resolved, either healed or as a lesson learned. Unfortunately for most, the original cause is often a cascading momentum of 'the domino effect', wherein effects are generated one from the other. Like rolls of wool unfolding, and creating a mess of unravelled wool, leaving you to try and find the beginning.

What Is the Cause and Effect?

There are four Universal laws that govern and impact each other in the stakes of cause and effect. There is, of course, the original rule of Cause and Effect, which determines this fact. 'Every cause has an ensuing impact, and in doing so creates more causes'. There is the law of correspondance, which explains, how patterns repeat themselves throughout the Universe and in life, The key is to recognise those patterns in our own lives so that we can take action either towards continuing with the positive ones or changing the habits that no longer serve us. There is the Universal law of Reincarnation. Hand in hand, they arrive as a log of records carried forward by our incoming and incarnating soul.

And last but not least, there is the Law of Compensation. This law explains, what you put out into the world will return to you. However, the Law of Compensation expands further because it says, whatever is in your heart will be returned to you. Words are powerful, but our emotions and beliefs are what powers our ability to manifest our thoughts into existence. Since this Universe is made up of living energy this law affirms the type of energy, we hold will be compensated with a like for like power. For example, if you do a good deed for another person, but you do it with resentment or in a negative way, what you receive is also resentment and anger. If you hold love in your heart when you do these deeds, then love will be returned as compensation.

Together these four edicts create opportunities and responsibilities, for each cause to be balanced, weighed and healed. The tentative subject of reincarnation is one that infers many discussions and creates lots of debates. However, what happens when your spirit, having spent the required amount of resting time, in the other environment where those who have left the physical plane reside after recapitulating and the weighing of opportunities and actions one undertook in life, is allowed to come back to Earth in a new body, with purpose.

The purpose? Is to continue the work already begun in its previous lifetimes, to heal and to complete any unfinished work. The karmic debt is merely energy, sometimes accumulated over several lifetimes where there has been an imbalance created during those times. Before coming into a new body, there has already been a discussion to determine what is needed by your soul to learn or experience. There is also a multitude of other souls who will have shared those previous lifetimes with you and who match your soul's ongoing requirements of balancing its karmic debt and who will become the players on your film set in this new life.

I wonder if we should consider the Religious conceptual ideal of 'purgatory' in a lesser more innocuous way. When we examine it more as a constant repetitive metaphor. For many of us, when we look at how causes and their ensuing rolling out effects, merely generate more causes which further impact our lives, until we heal and cease the continuous motion. Perhaps we should view purgatory, as a message which urges us to stop travelling in a loop. Purgatory then doesn't become the centralised theme as in the view of a 'Christian' hell. But explained better as an ongoing set of repeat circumstances, looping around and around on itself, until the archetypal serpent eventually swallows its tail and chokes on it.

The meaning of the serpent eating its tail is:
The ouroboros is an ancient symbol of a snake or serpent eating its tail, variously signifying infinity and the cycle of birth and death.

The Cycle of Life

Cycles are indications resulting from the map of our lives, and these indications show whether we are heading into a downward spiral, where we would suppose our lives are leaning towards a downward turn. This spiral takes us from a space of being bored, through its loops and twists and turns, of anger, hatred and jealousy to end up with feelings of insecurity, unworthiness, depression and powerlessness, allowing us to adopt the role of victim. The opposite is an upward spiral, where we acknowledge a feeling of contentment, and we are hopeful. We can express a positive belief in something, inferring the ability to be enthusiastic about being able to express joy, love, empowerment and freedom. There is another cycle, and one I feel has become lost along the way.

Not only do we find ourselves unceremoniously ejected from the 'Garden of Eden' but also since the original integrity of the first religion 'Mami Wata'. Became pilfered and re-branded and subsequently figureheaded by the Patriarchal worldview and its desire for power and domination over the Divine Feminine. It becomes the ill-formed and poorly constructed basis to the pervasive 'spiral of memory and belonging' and how its negative impetus has affected our very being as women especially.

There is also an unknown and unexplained feeling many of us experience. It leaves us in a state of void, one we cannot find a reason for why we feel something is missing. It is like having a memory block, or we think we have lost something, and we cannot determine what that is? There is such a sense of diasporic misalignment for many of us, not only within all of the slaves who were torn from their original homelands. Or those who wandered throughout the deserts of life, desperate to rediscover a new home, namely the Jewish Nation. But for many who still carry information within their cells and DNA strands, of an underlying feeling of being unsettled or being deprived of belonging to something, many of us cannot even express. A sense of memory and belonging is symptomatic of the purgatorial spiral, looping and turning in and around itself. One is primarily and unwittingly responsible for creating more and more causes and effects. There isn't anything more uncomfortable than a feeling of the unknown and a sense of disconnection when we do not know why? While this feeling exists and one we cannot explain why we feel this way, is a catalyst for how specific cause and effects are created in our lives. Especially when there isn't anything worse than not knowing why an uncomfortable feeling exists in the first place. It does, however, urge a need to find that cause, for no other reason than to save us from wandering throughout the abyss of the unknown. It furthers the purpose so many undertake the exploration urged on by an inexplicable need to find the answer in the many spiritual paths now available to all.

Furthermore, even in our spiritual exploration, many people still fall prey to unscrupulous teachers, some of whom can easily be classed as poachers or predatory. Waiting in the shadows to pounce on their vulnerable victims. Who in some cases are desperate to be loved, healed and feel valued once more. Here we find boundaries of trust are breached, creating further causes for the unsuspecting victim to endure and seek healing. Similarly, many try and attempt to find an expression of blissful reconnection once more. Seeking and in some cases never finding the loving arms of a Divine Protector, except only in an out of body journey of meditative exploration, where the veil of dimensions lifts and opens up to reveal its hidden treasures and gifts, indeed for some, a welcome distraction away from the reality of their lives.

Mistranslation and Theft Leads to a Sense of Loss

There is limited evidence that may explain, why we feel so profoundly a sense of soul loss. One which could explain why we carry the genes of disassociation and non-belonging. These factors contribute to who we have become in our present root race. The underlying sense we feel is fuelled by a cause, and this is the sense of great injustice, one which is for many of us unresolved. In-justice is something most people cannot let go of, and it isn't always associated with a need to forgive. But instead to reclaim something stolen and mistreated. It is the reason we are desperate to rediscover the truth, via reclaiming the incorruptible purity, which existed here on Earth at some point in our early existences. As a result of our unprecedented 'fall from grace' or the 'fall of man'. Has serendipitously placed us in a vacuum of trying to claw our way back into the grace of divine love. Hence the purgatorial arrival of the scales of justice and karmic board, which support us in clearing the debt and attaining karmic reward. Yet it all falls back to a need to gain legitimacy and justice.

Perhaps, I could offer one illustration of why this feeling exists, and it affects many women and men. There was a misrepresentation of translation when the original Matrilineal scrolls of the Serpent Priestesses were stolen and reconfigured. To give an example of how misinterpreting works, I refer to the bible and the following passage.

In the beginning, was the Word, and the Word was with God, and the Word was God. He was at the beginning with God. All things were made through him, and without him was not anything made that was made.

The inference here lies in the mistranslation of the original word which was **'logos'**, this was originally found in one of the scripts. By misinterpreting it, changes the whole of the above passage, when the word 'logos' is returned to the text.

The word 'logos' in Greek has several interpretations, such as:

'ground', 'plea', 'opinion', 'expectation', 'word', 'speech', 'account', 'reason', 'proportion', and 'discourse'.

Historical researchers have found that the translators selected the word 'logos' and then translated it to mean 'word'. This has misconstrued the correct meaning of the passage. For example, by replacing 'word' for 'reason'. Makes much better sense of both the passage's meaning and message.

In the beginning, was <u>Reason</u>, and the <u>Reason</u> was with God, and <u>Reason</u> was God. He was at the beginning with God. All things were made through him and with <u>Reason</u>, and without <u>Reason</u>, nothing was made.

When we examine why so many people are disconnected and have lost faith in religious practice, there is weight in understanding how these people have lost confidence due to manipulation by these human-made religions, merely because of its contrived need to dominate. Through this, we can determine why humankind has lost its sense of memory and belonging. It is observed when so much of the fundamental truth has been falsified.

Even with this one example, we can appreciate how much of the original script was mistranslated or rebranded and with purpose and engineering. Especially when a mere change of use of a single 'word', becomes more powerful when you are looking to snare followers for your new religion. Fear lies in the background of the impactive use of 'the word' when its meaning is deemed to be the word from God. Its suggested origin has a much more powerful way of trapping your audience. Therefore the 'word of God', was formulated into religious laws and was a sure way to attain obedience in society. As is the case within all areas of man's need for dominion, to control a mass of people, you need some extraordinarily believable and forceful laws, especially those which required civility and willingness, all sourced from a fear of an almighty being who holds the reigns to your life and death,

Without these statutes and processes in place, there would be no feasible way to gain power and formulate a hierarchy needed to establish their Kingdoms. In essence, Man allowed himself to be cast into a society of slavery, without the use of shackles and bars. Bondage comes in several forms, it comes in stealing another's freedom, and it also arrives in shackling a 'free' mind. Either way, the result is necessary when one needs to control the heathen.

Man-Made Religious Laws and Its Impact on Society

In the Ancient world and with the onset of these new patriarchal religions. Laws were established not only as a way of control but to ensure the masculine gained its power over the feminine. Laws were created not only in the Macrocosm of society but as an assurance of control was kept in the homes of its people.

Look and refresh yourself with the Ten Commandments, Moses supposedly received from God?

"You shall have no other gods before me.

"You shall not make for yourself a carved image or any likeness of anything that is in heaven above, or that is in the earth beneath, or that is in the water under the earth. You shall not bow down to them or serve them, for I the Lord your God am a jealous God, visiting the iniquity of the fathers on the children to the third and the fourth generation of those who hate me, but showing steadfast love to thousands of those who love me and keep my commandments.

"You shall not take the name of the Lord your God in vain, for the Lord will not hold him guiltless who takes his name in vain.

"Remember the Sabbath day to keep it holy. Six days you shall labour, and do all your work, but the seventh day is a Sabbath to the Lord your God. On it you shall not do any work, you, or your son, or your daughter, your male servant, nor your female servant, or your livestock, or the sojourner who is within your gates. For in six days, the Lord made heaven and earth, the sea, and all that is in them, and rested on the seventh day. Therefore the Lord blessed the Sabbath day and made it holy.

"Honor your father and your mother, that your days may be long in the land that the Lord your God is giving you.

"You shall not murder.

"You shall not commit adultery.

"You shall not steal.

"You shall not bear false witness against your neighbour.

"You shall not covet your neighbour's house; you shall not covet your neighbour's wife, nor his male servant, nor his female servant, nor his ox, nor his donkey, or anything that is your neighbour's."

An assured control was found and carried forth throughout hundreds of years, due to these commandments. In a way, doesn't it fall into the hands of a gross misrepresentation of the facts?

We could revisit the power of the word **reason**, to examine within itself the quality to raise man above all other creations. Yet with the ensuing new religions, all sense of **reason** left the building. Without purpose, humankind incurs soul loss brought on by the absence of faith, therefore losing the path to their innate spirituality. Even though religion dictates, to its brethren, that having faith is the only route to God. Any absence of Faith becomes detrimental to humankind, as we lose not only a dependency on our Higher God, but seemingly we lose our rational consciousness too.

Consequently, we begin the long journey of the seeker, continuing to make our own decisions using free will and choice. All because we lost the purpose for our existence and became enslaved to something which profoundly felt unnatural to our inner being. After all, there must be a purpose for everything, and if there isn't, we begin to lose our sense of memory and belonging.

Karmic Soul Loss

In that, the laws of cause and effect begin its journey from source throughout lifetimes to bite us in the proverbial bottom today. The endless purgatory started back in time when we adopted inauthenticity, and we gave up our ability to connect with Divinity ourselves. We lost faith because we could not feel the connection any longer. Instead, we used a middleman to do the work for us, and we stopped feeling it through our inner being when we allowed ourselves to be preached to and controlled by the laws of our religious overseers. We gave away our souls to them for our spiritual evolution and sacred connection. We found ourselves lost and adrift because we lost our purpose for being when our consciousness became the dominant and self-appraising ego. The purgatorial laws of Cause and Reincarnation stepped in as an attempt to help us find our way back through personal growth with a chance to balance the scales of justice. Add to this, the complication of free will promotes a further problem of choice. The very same only serves as a Russian roulette game of bringing forth a new cause or being left with merely the effect. Scientists inform us that man's ego comes and goes with each new life. However, after determining our spirit and soul is immortal, we could presuppose, the ego follows like a little lamb in and out of each earthly journey.

If you wonder why you are experiencing a specific set of circumstances in your life, the answer is now undoubtedly understood by the knowledge that somewhere in either this lifetime or a previous lifetime the original cause was established. The spirit recorded the experience, and how we endure these in this life is merely a test for us, hopefully, one we pass before we leave the confines of current life. Whether or not we feel we are persecuted by experience, or we are prone to types of misfortunes, other people do not seem to have, Our reward comes in the form of karmic reward. By the way, we acknowledge, grow and do good deeds to help other lost souls adrift in the sea of hopelessness. Until the time our spiritual karma far out weights its debt, and we are no longer a victim of weakness, reincarnation will continue to be offered as a way to learn eternal lessons.

After all, if we fully accept the fact, death doesn't exist. We can view reincarnation as a way of reforming and change. As we leave one life and continue into the next, we are indeed immortal beings. The ultimate aim, however, comes in finding a perfect way to help bring balance and order to a seemingly chaotic plethora of dimensional universes.

Universal laws help us navigate these perfect storms by helping us learn lessons from all our past lives. The experience, therefore, reveals specific hidden keys. Along with the realisation that we are the architects of our reality, due to an understanding of how these causes and effects create our existence. Finally, the last key is to ensure we do not repeat the same, purgatorial themes in our futures. Maybe I can add one further crucial idea, and this is to ask you to find your way back to establishing your faith, one which offers you a route to the Divine. In short, remember not to be influenced by the edicts or sermons of others, because you cannot be assured of a valid interpretation in their words. Find your way, by finding truth through the wisdom of sense and reason. After all, it is the perfect place to begin your spiritual journey back home.

Chapter 13

No Woman, No Cry! Part One

The age of woman is upon us once more, though is it the basis of the golden age?

After all, if this is so, then it cannot be based purely on woman dominance or feminist rights, in the sense of an old paradigm. The golden age should be a joint emergence of both Woman and Man, working and coexisting alongside each other, as true equals, but also as a complement of differences.

Each is owning and utilising their strengths and allowing the other to pick up the slack in the opposites weaknesses. This Utopia, is the route towards the golden age, though only by embodying love and trust and freedom as a personal guide. Utopia doesn't have segregation, or dominance or power-crazed individuals whose sole aim is to take as much from the precious earth resources as possible. No, this is a recipe for improvement and change and one which falls into the remit of love, trust and freedom. Because there isn't any change or learning to access if all we do is employ an old way of existing. The fight becomes immoral and bears little substance in the result. Yet, first, we need to know what the result should be.

Allow me to offer a tester of opinion, what would Utopia be and feel like, what is the long-term aim of such a golden age?

Utopia as in my idea of what Utopia would be:

Equality, all individuals, both animal and human, have a right to equality and respect.

The provision, everyone has a right to be provided with food, water, shelter and medical care.

Allowance, everyone takes responsibility for all provisions offered to them, ensuring they had enough, but not consuming more than needed.

Religion, Organised religions, including cults and dominion, would no longer exist.

Business, all businesses would become part of the whole, managed by the entirety and would work to provide the resources needed for everyone.

The government, all old frameworks of Government, would cease to be. In its place would be a return to local community responsibility and in the area of a central government would sit a counsel of both elders and young people.

Weapons, all weapons would cease to exist.

Education again, all old frameworks would be abolished. Replaced by teaching geared around broadening the horizons and minds of the students.

- Lessons would include Exploration into the Universe and in understanding dimensions, as well as science and creativity. Lessons would not be confined to a classroom, but instead, students would be allowed to experience the wonders and elements of nature. There would be many more field trips to explore museums, old churches and art galleries, to examine how art and sculpture depicted truth and legends.
- Her story would be taught as well as earlier models of humanity, via geography with an emphasis on different cultures around the world.
- All tests and exams would be eradicated, and all of this would ensure freedom of mind would allow greatness and creativity to emerge.

However, before any dreaming of Shangri-La can commence, there is a deep and profound action to be both acknowledged and healed. This issue lies in the very deep crevices of women and the many hundreds of injustices she beholds inside her karmic river. From the first moment in time, where she became dominated, and her freedom and gifts were stolen, way back to the time when the first whiff of a patriarchal takeover became evident. When all the Priestesses and temple aides, were placed under threat of extinction unless they surrendered to the rough hand. Women's lives significantly changed and without any hope of equality offered again, until much later in a more evolved time. Even apart from the women who once held stature and importance, to those women who became threatened and were suddenly forced to walk three feet behind their men. Womankind and her sisters, suddenly became (and not by choice), slaves and concubines to their husbands, fathers and other male family members.

Can we dare to imagine what it must have been like, to suddenly move from having stature and a primary relationship to the Divine? To suddenly becoming thrust into a role of quiet protest, whereby you became your Father or husbands property, having to ask for permission to exist. There are conflicting accounts of how more women than their male counterparts converted to Christianity when it was first introduced. Though looking deeper into this fact, it seems like it was the higher born woman who readily adopted this new religion. Not necessarily for the sacredness, it offered, but merely to keep a foothold in the senates and society. Though looking at early Christianity, through the Abrahamic faiths, which followed the path of Judaism, this evidence shows that women were not viewed as equals, due to a male-orientated desire for power and authority. Our Ancient world being male-dominated, crept over into the New Church and its ideal of woman's roles, perhaps this is purely attributed to the fact of ancient women were not educated, which hindered their ability for standing in society and from becoming leaders. Though, the 'word', became law, as did the ability to transcribe the word so that it could spread far and wide. This alone separated men from women, as it was the man's role to do this work.

In their roles, whether this accounted for women who held the position of Priestess in the Ancient world or one who grew up in an agricultural background, most literature, other than the main holy books, detail only a handful of essential women, in his chronicles. I read one account, which stated, 'women who were highly influential during the rise of Christianity, have been airbrushed out of history'. It is an argument, not only the women who were airbrushed out of history hold. In the same way, the earlier position of the Mami Wata Priestesses, or the Serpent Priestesses and Sibyls have all been eradicated from the his-story books. Along with the truth and wisdom of our lineage and abilities.

Even now, Islamic women do not worship alongside their men. Their sacred worship is carried out in separate buildings or even in the home. What message does this give or how does this affect women, who can't worship in the same place. Then again, what does this say about women who seem to allow this to continue?

Looking back to the women's role in the Ancient World, it seems there are differing accounts of how they lived. For example, in Ancient Egypt, women had a lot of freedom, being able to own property as well as having the ability to divorce their spouses. Work in the home was a primary function. Though there is also evidence of women doctors and even a women Pharoah. In Ancient Greece, women held much more significant positions, from taking part in religious ceremonies, to managing the finances. Many helped their husbands on the land and kept their homes, and some worked as merchants. Girls fared better than some of their counterparts across the world in the stakes of education. This lead to more women becoming writers, philosophers and scientists.

As I write this, it is evident to me of quite a small portion of influential women, who had status across the ancient world. Maybe there is an essential point to make here, and it is built around an idea, of how women have faired in the stakes of equality now and back then. Of course in the western world, we can celebrate how much more freedom and opportunities we have, though as I write this, and I feel apologetic for even having to write this down. However, there is still an underlying disproportionate number across the modern world who, have different freedoms available to them. Of course, we have to account for each other's circumstances. Yet, women, in general, are not equal or do they readily have the same opportunities as men. It isn't a Women's-Right statement I'm making either, as I believe it hails much further back than this. I feel it derives from a legacy of how somehow along the human evolutionary chain, women became feared and viewed suspiciously, due to the miracle of creative power and creation we hold within us. Perhaps it is the way we command a quiet inner strength that becomes threatening to some males. It would have been far more problematic to the male in the ancient world. Women were not given any honour for being able to produce life from their bellies. Let alone stand alongside the male to provide and offer food to keep their families alive. Assuming this and looking at how much authority women held in their roles as Priestess or Oracles was imperative to the ancient kingdom figureheads. Again, became even more of a demasculinisation of the male. Women always and still do have an innate ability to create bridges, by their capability to stay quiet and observe the bigger picture.

To understand this issue better, perhaps it is necessary to revert to a central theme. As well as following the role of the feminine in the Ancient World, more in the way of a non-modernistic approach.

Our mindset would then be in a better place to interpret how women were viewed, not in the way of a battle between sexes, but rather as fitting into a set of criteria components. These being, freedom (as in not a slave) holding status, via the ability to work or marriage. Foreigner or barbaric heathen, Slave or Servant. Therefore one's status was measured and defined within its country of habitation. How you fit into the hierarchical social scale, is determined by your class, yet in saying this, it is right to point out the economic scales were still tipped towards the role of the male in his environment of politics, power, law and the army. Within these establishments, it was an essential aim of the man to make his mark and therefore be measured in his successes. As far back in the Ancient World, men were seen as superior, though not merely for their intelligence, but their manliness and strength.

For women and this was purely down to circumstances, you either worked the land, kept the home or if your situation allowed, you would be drawn towards art and literature. As time and humanity evolved from being primarily an agricultural nation into a more industrialised country. The masculine still valued and even does the same today, his physical strength, aggressive combativeness and ability to build, all of which are due to physical stamina. The female's role was and again still is around the need to procreate. An important part, when you take into account early childhood mortality rates and shorter life expectancy to around the late 40s. A woman played her role to ensure society continued to grow by giving birth. However, the length of time it took for a baby to gestate within the womb, would mean women were unable to become actively involved in society.

Where women did hold power, as mentioned in an earlier chapter, and this was in the temples and the homes. Of course, In religious history, this became short-lived, with the rampacious overthrowing of feminine responsibility within the ancient religious institutions. The masculine might and power of Islam, Judaism and Christianity, became the early saboteurs and enforcers of gender prejudice. Shamefully, it is a clear indication women had to give their ability away to continue to survive, and for some to guarantee this, they exiled themselves. There again, this became the beginning of gender debasement to ensure women, no longer rose to hold vital status still. Unquestionably, this was the fate for those women who did stay, as they became subjects of ridicule and torture as death seemingly followed as a warning to any other women who may have had ideas to fight the Patriarchal overthrow.

Nobody knew much different back then, let alone be able to question the unequal might of both strength and indoctrination of these new religions. Even Queens in power couldn't challenge this might, and it is a primordial requirement to find genuine ways to survive this apparent new dawn of patriarchal, control and acquisition. The indication comes from this actual point in history, as women became fragile and unable to fight it head-on. Another essential aspect to add is the underlying reasons behind the male's insistence on complete domination and power which drove patriarchy. The masculine need for control has always resided in his longing to be the greatest nation, to have the most wealth, to be unchallenged and unbeatable by his enemy. These factors contribute to the status and awareness of society. For that reason, there is a much more profound desire for man to attain, and this is to be equal to or to be seen as a God. One thing man has unachieved in his new dawn, in both the Ancient and Modern world is God-hood. Back in the times of Atlantis, they indeed tried hard to attain this.

Even after the flood and devastation of Atlantis, it is said a group of people migrated around 2,200 BC and arrived at the Land of Shinar, known as Sumer (now Iran). The story does, of course, bring in the story of Noah, building an Ark to escape the great deluge. However, the biblical account of the Tower of Babel is found in Genesis 11. It was said, some of Noah's descendants who survived the flood, settled within the plains of Shinar. During this time, they had developed a disconnection from God and began planning to erect a high tower. They desired to build themselves a prosperous and renowned city, with a tower that easily could reach the heavens. Their aim was urged on entirely by their aggrandisement and ego. However, the causal desire was to be able to meet God and become one with the Highest, but what drove this need was their arrogance, and the Tower of Babel was more akin to being a monument to a desire for greatness and prestige. The tower was to be a place of worship. The tale of the tower concludes with the Most-High becoming displeased at humanities arrogance. He proceeded to offer judgement on this, and he decided to scatter the people and to give them all their language, from here on they would become separated and settle in new locations and on new lands.

Genesis 11

"Now the whole earth had one language and the same words. And as people migrated from the east, they found a plain in the land of Shinar and settled there. And they said to each other, 'Come, let us make bricks and burn them thoroughly'. And they had brick for stone, and they had tar for mortar. And they said, 'Come, let us build ourselves a city and a tower whose top reaches to the heavens. And let us make a name for ourselves, lest we are scattered over the face of the whole earth'.
Then Yahweh came down to see the city and the tower that humankind was building. And Yahweh said, 'Behold, they are one people with one language, and this is only the beginning of what they will do. So now nothing that they intend to do will be impossible for them. Come, let us go down and confuse their language there so that they will not understand each other's language'. So Yahweh scattered them from there over the face of the whole earth, and they stopped building the city. Therefore its name was called Babel, for there Yahweh confused the language of the entire earth, and there Yahweh scattered them over the face of the whole earth."

This illustration of the endless desire man has to become equal with Divinity is merely one story out of many accounts of history. There is a darker side to this, and it always resides in his need to embody and use supernatural powers. A longing to be able to manipulate and influence by way of magical incantations, powerful weapons and magical tools. Throughout his-story, there are illustrations of Man seeking to find the answer or to discover these sacred artefacts and tools. From the Ancient World to the Romans, to the Catholic Institution to Hitler and possibly hundreds of others in between. From the moment women became the keeper of the sacred mysteries, and she could do the divinations and counsel straight from the holy libraries. She became a threat, and her position became precarious.

The initial seeding of Africa and its portals, where the Iyami come and go in and out of human form. Again became a target, a hotspot for those who wanted to find this sacred treasure. Under the guise of looking for gold and diamonds, it was the Europeans, the Portuguese, the Dutch, the French and the English who came to pillage the richness of Africa, stealing precious life and ripping it from its homeland, in the guise of human cargo and the onset of the slave trade. Upon accomplishing, this resulted in removing the Africans and enslaving them to suffer lifetimes of cruelty and hard labour. Yet by taking them from their land allowed the Europeans to scavenge for the rich pickings, as now they were unattended and available for stealing.

Behind all of this and easily shielded by escapades of the slave traders, there would be another poacher of human existence. Possibly disguised as an archaeologist or even missionary, he aimed to find the sacred texts and truth of where we came from and how to build a bridge back there. It is still going on today, call it by many names, the result is the same.

For us as women, some are desperate to reclaim our rightful place, and this is to guard the bridge between the Material World and other Dimensions and finally recover our route to Divinity. To be able to safeguard this without fear of reprisal or being ridiculed. There is also a secondary requirement, and I will discuss this in a later chapter. We want to be able to stand alongside the men, as a complement of differences as well as being able to call on each other's strengths as a means to bring balance back to Earth. To bring equality of the genders is not necessarily something man can grant. It is attained by both sexes demanding society changes, to ensure all of life can prosper. Otherwise, we will only see waste as we allow growth to continue with the barbaric treatment of women and her body. Racism is alive and flourishing in the way some men view the idea of the feminine. There is wisdom in truth. No nation can survive unless every human being has the same rights and liberties. Without which, we will all remain as slaves to our masters!

But first, before this can happen, we have to heal ourselves from lifetimes of imbalance and karma.

Chapter 14

No Woman, No Cry! Part Two

The River Runs Deep!

To regain balance, when all around you is in disarray, and you witness at every turn a state of chaotic disorder, whether this is made manifest around the Globe or is mirrored in the microscopic world of one's personal life. Is a feat of somewhat epic proportion and a Mount Everestian challenge! Whether life serves its delicacies to you on a golden platter, or one made of paper is immaterial in the end. Because unless we understand what we have to heal and attend to, it can become lost in a sea of no hope and is filed under meaningless, formless energy.

We may be able to put into words how we feel, for example, 'I feel angry, hurt and confused' or 'I feel empty, under pressure and in pain' or 'I am suffering, I am sad and detached'. Is all well and good, but we need to appreciate the what and the why, and how this underpins the emotions and feelings we embody. Yet if these are held, the underworld river is itself lost in the eternities of times gone by, and this river is everywhere at the same time, and eventually, all channels merge into one. Is quite an enormous energy to hold. The river I speak of is an internal force and a catalogue of our past life experiences, all held within the sacred libraries of our soul. How these surface and replay in this life becomes the foundation of our identity, and how the events we meet head-on, affect who we become.

Today, mental illness is common, and there aren't many people who have not been affected in some way by this modern-day #hastag. The waiting rooms of Dr's surgeries are full of people, desperate to get help and relief. The so-termed Mental facilities are full to brimming with patients categorised into boxes of similar symptoms. Managed by pharmaceutical concoctions of drugs and pills, and offered many different therapies, such as Cognitive Behavioural Therapy, Dialectical Behavioural Therapy, Interpersonal Therapy, Mindfulness-based Therapies, Psychodynamic Therapy, Group Therapy, Emotion-Focussed Therapy, Family Therapy and Psychotherapy. Naming a few on offer to try and get someones mental state functioning once more. When I say 'functioning again', I mean, in a suitable state of being able to live within the confines of society once more. Perhaps not in the same way of those who can tread the boards of work, rest, and play, types of people, but at the very least of being able to live outside of the hospital grounds, under supervision, but alone.

To reason, mental health and the ascending figures of those who suffer is impossible from the clinical explanation and perspective. However, if I could offer some light on the spectrum of this little-known rise in phenomena, from a spiritual and sacred perspective, maybe there could be some light in the tunnel?

As a non-expert, I place mental health as being filed under six headings, which, of course, affect modern-day society. I'll go into a more profound spiritual detail in a moment.

The Six Principles of Depression and Anxiety

The Surface Principle

Sometimes when you awake from your slumber, or perhaps you have endured a sleepless or disturbed night, and you have had endless dreams. You feel somewhat down, or there is a lower feeling of negation around you, one you cannot explain. Perhaps you had a great nights sleep, and in the middle of your busy day, suddenly you are overcome by feeling low, and again there is no apparent reason for it. To explain more, it is a sudden and unexplained impression, like someone covered you with a black veil. Your mood drops, your spirit falls, and the only thing you can describe is how flat you feel.

The Global Principle

The state of the world and its nations is in turmoil, and the weather is in a constant state of unprecedented fluctuation away from the norm or season. There are unique events of rampaging fires sweeping throughout acres of the earth and deluges and floods which come from nowhere. The inner Earth and its erupting volcanoes, land and mudslides are far more common, making us feel very uncomfortable. The World leaders seem inept and incapable of caring, and there are visible expressions of darkness and violence laid bare on the TV and throughout social media. How this affects us is either personally or from an unknown air of empathic energy is imbued as we sit back and watch it happen. The energetic approach is unexplainable to many, yet to fully appreciate it, we need to review the chapter on cause and effect. Energy is powerful and whether its power is derived from mass fear or mass exhalation, believe me when I say, it spreads across the globe from person to person like an invisible cloak and unless you are completely closed off, you will feel it at some level.

The Threat to Freedom or Life Principle

This threat to our well-being has come with the turning of a new year, 2020. The year of the pandemic, lockdown, restrictive freedom and conspiracy theories. The unthinkable happened, a nightmare unfolded and arrived at everyone's door. Some have experienced a long stint of illness, which is a direct result of the pandemic. Others have become locked away in their homes out of fear, while the whole world has had their freedoms and liberties curtailed by their governments. Everyone's routines, working life, self-medicating, social interactions have ceased, with the majority of shops in lockdown closure and all restaurants, pubs and sporting venues and gyms are closed. Everything we did to amuse, distract or which added to our wellbeing disappeared. Suddenly and inexplicably brutally, our sane sense of lifestyle vanished. Many people lost their loved ones, either from a direct result of the pandemic or from a long-standing illness. Many people have taken their lives because they could no longer cope with the lack of freedom or from the fear something like a pandemic enforces. Whether we trusted the way our governments dealt with it, or we have become suspicious of the underlying reason for it all. The effect and fallout from this pandemic made many of us feel uneasy, and we do not feel comfortable with how it is managed and the options offered by the medical facilities. This principle, which would also be present in any war situation, has knocked us off our laurels of security and trust.

The Reality Principle

Life, your life and most lives are one of a never-ending set of events of a complicated nature. Whatever you do, you are unable to escape from the hole you continually fall inside. Call it bad luck or misfortune, call it 'not being able to catch a break'. These catapulting events eventually knock you off course. Conceivably it manifests in your relationships, where you cannot sustain or commit to a loving union, or you are unable to get a good job or even keep a job, which would allow you to pay the bills and tariffs required by society. Perhaps you have had a difficult childhood, which has propelled you into an unsustainable living arrangement, or, you have found yourself walking down a criminal path.

Sometimes other experiences happen in life; for example, you are betrayed by someone you trusted. Maybe this betrayal occurred in the workplace or another area of your life. Whatever misfortune happened within this reality effect, can and will become too difficult for you to handle.

197

The Social Principle

The social principle ties into the reality effect. However, it stands autonomously on its own. Because when we attempt to measure who and how we are, unrealistically against someone else, this in itself becomes a mountain we never get to the top of, unless we make a sacrifice. If we attempt to strive to be the 'best' by trying to match the standards of another person, is something we cannot sustain, all we achieve here is to give away our precious life force by cloning oneself to become a version of them. We are who we are, our personality is moulded by our soul, and our spirit has lived hundreds of lifetimes. However, if it's an identity you seek, then, of course, this can be bought. Whether spending money on plastic surgery or cosmetics and clothes. Will this make you feel socially accepted or wanted or even let you experience love? Of course, this remains to be seen.

Everything can be bought they say, however, if you require peace and self-realisation, then you will have to work for it. While this is the case, there are, of course, many who fall out of the false illusion of social expectation and achievement. When someone doesn't fit in because of not being funny enough, or intelligent enough or pretty enough or thin enough. Can make this person feel ostracised and unaccepted by the group or whole. It leads to further social pitfalls, for example; loneliness, withdrawal and sometimes bullying. Whenever we become apart from the group, there is a danger of falling into the underworld, underworld realms, here the Ego mind takes precedence and causes untold damage to our self-esteem.

The Underworld, underworld requires some explanation. There is a misconception about the underworld, and this has only just been enlightened to me. The underworld meant one thing, an unknown place not in physical reality, yet one we sank to when we were dealing with our shadows and unhappiness. We envisage a deep and dark rocky terrain, leading to an underground cavern, where we reside when we need to lick our wounds and where our lost soul parts become trapped. Stories and Legends have steered us from understanding the actual meaning of descending into life. While we await a new incarnation, we rest in the other realms, until the right circumstances for our incarnating life are made available. Maybe these are the parents who provide us with the necessary qualities of lifestyle, or the location is suitable for our needs. Either way, we wait until all the right set of corresponding circumstances are in place before we enter into a new physical body. As bodies of light, comprised of a glimmering soul and all its essences of previous incarnations, are housed within our lineage heaven. Then when everything is ready, we fall from our heavenly plane into the seeds of our parents while they procreate. Waiting until our new organic body grows around our glittering soul. The Fall from lineage heaven is falling into the underworld, and it is how the upper worlds denote Earth-life. The underworld-underworld is the place we fall further when we are working with our shadow aspects and wounds.

Reality Principles and Depression and Anxiety

To summarise these principles mentioned above is to look at them as life lessons. Yes, some do seem like they are unavoidable, and in a way, they can be, as cause and effect come ever more to the forefront. Of course, we have choices to make every step of the way. And of course, we all make the wrong decisions about things also. I also admit how important our upbringing is to who we become as adults. Nature or nurture is quantifiable enough of a basis for any fabulous or stressful life. Again, I also need to revert to the needful part of the soul and its requirement to learn specific life lessons. However, when one is in the deep, dark hole of depression, no placation will work, as it will merely come across as dismissive. Yet, what does pull some out of the indelible hole? When for others, nothing is there to save them? Perhaps it is because certain people get lost along the way and become victims of the game. Either way, there is no one cap fits all here, yet all any of us can achieve is to try our damnedest to regain balance in our lives and to defeat the chaos around us. Balance is found while attending to our physical, mental, emotional and spiritual bodies needs. All of which require equal and fair attention.

The Unknown Principle from Origin to Separation
The last principle and one often overlooked

A river meanders with a more profound stirring inside so many of us, whether we are on the path of 'spiritual awakening'. Or merely living our lives. There is an innermost uneasiness one which cannot and will not be sated whatever we try. No one understands why there is such a strange and unsettled feeling, and we often try and account for it by initially attaching it to feeling unwell or perhaps we have a virus of some sort.

Symptoms include nausea, depression, aches and pains, panic attacks and restlessness and our visit to our Dr or Alternative Health Practitioner will help place a temporary plaster over the symptoms. Though like any other provisional remedy, it is short-term and merely distractionary. As symptoms grow more robust, eventually turning from the physical to a more troubling inner disquiet. Before long the symptoms advance from matter into the neuropathways of the mental body, Here our captain, the ego-mind attempts to analyse its emotional turbulence, as we head down the 'surface' manifestations of abandonment, loss, anger, and confusion. The natural progression from this point is to examine with a fine toothcomb, the past events of life, childhood experiences, adolescent trauma and adult sorrows and mishaps.

Yet, what if the feeling spewing forth from inside the turbulence of our river, comes from an event long, long ago, aeons ago and It was cataclysmic, and it changes who we are as women (or men). Yet, it became etched inside the cells and DNA of our soul's sacred library? To glean any sense of relief and resolution from this resides in the bottomless lake of self-evolution. Yet to understand the route of humanity, and in its evolution in more detail, we must return to the very beginning!

Primordial Adam Kadmon

From the primordial first incarnation of Adam Kadmon (original blueprint). To who we are in the fifth incarnation of the human form, comes from a massive leap across a void of ever-changing expressions of self-realisation. We are no longer in the original way our Creator intended for us as humans to be. The original Adam Kadmon was the first stage, an age of man, a conjoined masculine and feminine of the latter more commonly known Adam and Eve, not separate but entrenched together as Adam Kadmon. To accept this original blueprint requires us to further take Earth as a created planet and how it became manifest time and time again. Call it as the conspirative theorists do, 'an experiment', wherein each time earth was created and uncreated is merely down to failed existences of human mismanagement. In the beginning, Adam Kadmon held within itself both positive and negative expressions as his potentiality.

This first original Adam is undefined and superimposed as a single primordial thoughtform, without any separation or division. He parallels the highest source of consciousness in man and is combined as total unity with the light of the Infinite (or, Most-High), He is identified as the entire Universe and the soul and essence of all things, an essential ideal of linking God, the Creator to Man and the Earth. Separation begins to happen here, as Adam divides and breaks away from the light into individual qualities, separation begins to inform the body as a separation of the heart and the stomach via the bridge of the solar plexus, it is here at the bridge the separation, becomes bodily permeated. A space many of us hold or cross our hands over when we feel vulnerable or under attack.

As Adam held the power of creation within itself, he could create thought into physical matter. Even while conjoined to the Creative principle, he could work with both negative and positive and create and shape it into form. From this form the infamous Garden of Eden was designed, it was to hold everything man needed to sustain and entertain himself. The Garden of Eden was never found in the third dimension. The fall of man aligns itself with the truth of Man's body becoming divided from Adam Kadmon into two separate parts, one positive and one negative, this eventually entered into the organic animal body known as man. Here we see the evolving state of man from the original blueprint into body form, yet the spirit itself didn't enter the physical body at this stage. When the spirit did come into Adam Kadmon first, still beholding the masculine and feminine in one body. It was in this period, the fall of man by way of a division took place, a separation of ego and consciousness into two separate parts, The masculine and the feminine, creating a two-gendered and two different polarities of a new race of humans. The evolution of the next blueprints arrived from Adam Kadmon into the subsequent generation Adam and Eve complex.

In the Garden of Eden, man and woman stayed here to learn. Here the legendary Tree of life legend comes into the picture. In their infancy, to eat the fruit from the tree of life would only result in hastening man's fall even more significantly, by creating an uncertain state in which to live on Earth while embodying the knowledge of the twelve fruits of the Tree of Life of good and evil, or better determined as positive and negative.

Then again if the Tree of life and the tree of knowledge is the mythical, archetypal expression of evil and wisdom. The mythological use of the word fruit would be not to eat any fruit which had seeds in it. As seeds create ideas and thoughts and then questions? In the Garden of Eden, man enjoyed love, joy, peace, patience, kindness, goodness, faithfulness, gentleness and self-control. However, in this perfect place of oneness as its expression of divinity, would soon become a challenge and not conducent to the earth 'experiment' which was to follow. Therefore Man wanted to know more, and when Eve ate the fruit, it was she who observed the knowledge and wisdom as her sense of self became more durable. Should we look at the fruit of knowledge as an awakening and the start of a realisation of not only the enormous power of divinity and what could be possible and made manifest? After all, this is the version that backs up the belief in the abilities and gifts of those first prophetesses and Sibyls. The symbolic legend of Adam and Eve and how by consuming the fruit from the tree of knowledge has become debased by untruths. Devised to blame women and to define her as sinful and unclean, which only plays further to allow the violators complicit reasoning for how he has served to keep her in as a fear-driven subservient slave. Why would the Creator punish her so? After all, it was to be Adam and Eve in the second cycle, who would bring forth the experimental human evolution. Fast forward to Earth and how humans burst forth from the minerals and first began to learn and survive. Taught solely by Mami Wata, the beings who came from out of the sea and how these became the serpents of knowledge and substance of human survival.

Myth or perhaps truth? Eventually, it was Man who became undermined by the Mami Wata priestesses powers. As man evolved and became more capable and powerful in his own right. He no longer needed help from Mami Wata to survive. The focus was placed towards these first women priestesses and counsels, advocates of Mami Wata who knew the wisdom and truth as shared by Mami Wata. It was she who not only revered the supremacy of the serpent and used it in both arts and as protectors of their temples. (Symbolically snake was used everywhere as an authoritative interpretation of sacredness in many ancient cultures; its symbolism meant wisdom, death, resurrection, fertility and procreation, all of these are feminine attributes).

However, all the holy books written by man has condemned the serpent as a chaotic evil power, linking it firmly with the underworld and Satan. It again is only to demean and usurp not just women but anyone who worked to embrace the ancients truths. It is stated in the Christian Bible, how they trampled on the head of the serpent. To demonstrate suppressing the true meaning of the mystery teachings throughout Babylonia, Chaldea and Africa. As we know, many of the ancient libraries in Greece were set alight in an attempt to eradicate all traces of truth. Women from the moment Eve took the first bite and became the keeper of the mysteries and all those who followed in human form in her footsteps, held a precarious position. As the evidence suggests in all of these holy books, how Man, the mighty hunter swept through the ancient cities with one aim in mind. It was to find the truth held in the mystery schools and then destroy them. Even when he couldn't extinguish all of them, he began to write a distorted account of its mysteries and truths.

To better understand how we, as women experience such feelings of injustice and how this leaves such a bad taste in our mouths today, has to come from 100,000 years ago when the first injustice occurred. To explain this more in detail, let us backtrack to the beginning once again.

A Quick Backtrack and Recap

The Mami Wata traditions of a powerful and commanding matrilineal group of healers, seers and prophetesses, known as the Sibyls or Snake Goddesses, were observed as the original religion on Earth. How this came about was from a direct bloodline link to the Divine African Queen Mother. She is the Primordial Mother of the Cosmos, Sun and Moon, and she can change from male to female at need. She birthed the 'Forces of Nature' or 'Orisha', who could manifest into human form from the spirits. These forces of nature, supervise the morality and service of man and creature here on this planet.

Part of the Water Pantheon of Deities is 'Mami Wata', known throughout the Ancient and modern world as Oannaes, Dagon, Mami, Ishtar, Atergatis and Poseidon. Through these Deities, The Divine African Queen Mother could manifest and take form. The Mami Wata Pantheon propagated the seeds of humanity, left by the Divine Mothers Iyami in the water and then as humans evolved on land, they began to teach them social order and survival etc. They became the origin of the first religion here on Earth and held a sacred authority as well as being the spiritual architects of civilisation. The first offspring of Mami Wata began in Africa, Egypt or Khem, Mesopotamia (Sumeria), Asia Minor (Turkey) and India. Later spreading outwards to the Greek and Roman Cultures. The women who were the crucial heads of the Ist religion were the Sibyls or Snake Goddesses who were arbitrary in their importance and ability to receive the divine logos and truth from Iyami. Via translation, they would inform the Kings and Heads of State. Via their role of supremacy and prominence, throughout the Ancient World, they were the original Ark of the Covenant. Though instead of a chest made of Acacia wood and inlaid with gold. Everything was made manifest through an object known as the Holy Mound or (Womb of God). It was this sacred mound responsible for birthing the Deities.

Woman's Pain

From holding such prominence in the Ancient World, the ensuing degradation soon came as the Patriarchal Jews, Islamists and Christians brought to serve their need for ownership and supremacy of the Gods. The once morality of society was no more as they brought with them a degeneration built around corruption and the decline of the significant Divine truth and wisdom. From this point in her story, became overshadowed and overlayed by marauding masculinity brimming with Testosteronic fervour. They aimed to appropriate and commandeer everything sacred and sacrosanct. It was here, pain and suffering were embodied in woman's bodies and their DNA. As they had to stand by and watch the primordial Matrilineal line become eradicated and desecrated.

This injustice isn't merely to do with Woman's survival, but instead, it is proliferated in a profound sense of loss of self-reverence. Manifested as imprisonment and raped of her initial standing of being a creatrix of life and beholder of the sacred mysteries. Throughout the ensuing centuries, the feminine took second place to men. They were hounded and tormented for any feminine gifts of clairvoyance, herbalism and carers of the sick. The Female form became nothing more than an appendage to the male as he viewed her merely as a pleasure palace and mother of his need to produce an heir. From then and still, in some modern-day circles, women are even ridiculed and belittled for displaying any ethereal abilities. Today as many suffer, rape, abuse, sexual assault, inappropriate talk, many still need to fight for equal pay and rights. Perhaps we should be exploring why we are so compliant? Or instead, we should be examining the connection to the river of karma that courses throughout our DNA and how this impacts who we are today.

There is a simple idea to ponder on, and it asks us to determine how it is possible to suppose our Divine Ancestral Mothers or Iyami and her consorts. Could condone our degradation from being a vital component in the Divine Matriarchal Religions born out of the initial seeding, to end up with the Divine turning their back on all women in favour of patriarchal racism?

In highlighting this as probable cause for much of the spoiling of our deeply seated karmic rivers full of lifetimes of experiences and events. It is undoubtedly time to begin the healing of our feminity and allow ourselves the space to let this unfold. Because if we do this, and even ignore what a mammoth task it seems to be, we shall find our freedom and become far more at peace with ourselves again.

Peace comes when we realise the men who love unconditionally and support us will forever be by our side in any subsequent battles.

By healing the feminine essence, it will then cease to manifest itself in the depreciation of our spirits. The first rule, however, begins as the New Dawn approaches and we no longer allow Man in his archetypal role of ecclesiastical figurehead to perform all our initiatory rites and to enable him to sermonise and preach for our morality. We as women will never be at peace until we reclaim the gold of inner sacredness and further understand how to learn how to perform our sacred duty. By retrieving those gifts, the patriarchy assumed responsibility for and then turned off out of fear of reprisal. We now claim back by way of understanding they had no right to do so.

From this day forward, we call our Divine Ancestral Mothers to stand behind us and watch over us, as we undertake the steps of healing required, to then finally revoke all they stole and misused, as we claim our birthrights.

Ashe

Chapter 15

Introducing the Divine Masculine

We talk a lot about the Divine Feminine and how she lost her status, power and divinity over the aeons. Though little is spoken about the Divine Masculine and where he lost his sense of self, having become overlayed with countless atrocities throughout his lifetimes. These have understandably disconnected him far from his original 'Adam Kadmon', purity of self.

Views on this subject may well infer about how the Divine Masculine had become ignored in his divine right. Yet legacy and patriarchal history would attest to this. Especially if for no other reason to state how unjust this statement may be. By its proclamation alone, we must agree how the masculine has taken centre stage for at least 3,500 years. In both influential roles within the hierarchies of human-made religions, governments and industry. We do not have to stretch our imaginations too far back to the Victorian age when women authors had to assume a male name, to get their books published! Though bitterness isn't the basis of this chapter, as, within these words, we should seek to discover where the Divine masculine has gone?

Who Is the Divine Masculine?

He, while in the role of equality, doesn't embody a need to 'be in charge', he, embraces his feminine partner. Whereby he doesn't need to own or chattel her in any way, he will not use his strength of power to threaten her ability either. More importantly, he compliments her as the Captain of their ship. Though they are different in every way, they know there is a divine plan at stake, one which is more significant than both of them. Yet within this plan, he also understands at the same time he is the creator for his Divine Feminines creativity, he is the solid rock, and she is the Universe in its expressive aspect. They are partners each one a part of the whole, he is the architect of life in the material, and in the unseen world. Yet she is the weaver of both creation and destruction, as she weaves the fates and destinies of their lives, he is the one to pull her back if she strays off the path of purpose. She too will do the same for him, if she feels his architectural mind beginning to stretch itself unnecessarily overly. Together they are a force to be reckoned with, especially while they steer and weave together, nothing can touch them, the power of divine breath runs through them both.

The Divine Masculine Struggles

Presently, here on Earth, the Divine Masculine hasn't reached its full potential yet, and the reason is contained within his seeds. His ancestral legacy became compromised by his actions and behaviours though long gone through aeons. He has inherited strands of karmic debts leftover from his ancestral bloodlines. Especially those who were involved in the atrocities of wars, violence and subjugation. These invisible debts course through his DNA, like a hidden river of influential memory. Its deeds unknown yet felt in the core of his being. Knowledge of his genealogy escapes him, yet he spends part of his life, searching and seeking the elusive golden fleece. Looking to ease himself, byways of prospering and status. His masculine role has become confused by the need to succeed, and he hopes to find within his success and achievements a sense of peace. Yet, he is missing knowledge and understanding of the divine bigger picture. Divinity requires partnership, and it involves balance, this is only found when the masculine becomes the divine consort to his female. Until then, he will stay lost, lacking true potential, and he will remain in the third-dimensional construct of purgatorial separation and judgement.

As he fights to soar, he is measured and rewarded either favourably or punished. His archetypal highs and lows, become his foundation of being, he has difficulty surfing seamlessly through the tides of life. Instead, he seeks distraction and medication to ease his furrowed brow and disease. Wine, women and song, would be the old fashioned way to self medicate his loss of self. Then again, the modern world has evolved far more in its offerings of self-sabotage and self-styled aggrandisements. The stakes of satisfaction are set at a much higher bar today, as wine, women and song, have long gone as they cannot satisfy the unsatisfied. Alcohol, drugs, gambling, the dark web, food, animal abuse and increased sexual appetites are the food to fuel the lack in the self. One which affects the lost feminine also, yet the worrying aspect to all this lies in the question, 'when is enough... enough?' 'When will the unstable ever become satisfied?' Or will they continue to search for darker and darker ways to medicate their voids?

There again, for some men, there is a lack of a fatherly role in their lives, there are not enough men who can father their sons. They too have become victims to this bottomless pit of the abyss, lost while trying to find the elusive golden fleece or the simplicity of an answer, 'who am I and do I matter'. It leaves many male children to be brought up by their mothers, who do a sterling job of mothering their fatherless children. However, what remains is sons who throughout their teenage years and into adulthood, end up perceiving relationships with the feminine in the wrong way. Rather than seeking a partner or divine consort, they look to be continually mothered throughout their adult lives, by their wives and partners. The archetypal fixation with a women's breasts is a sincere seeking of nurturing and comfort to sate their troubled souls.

Perhaps this is the inherent problem with society today, as it has taken the masculine role throughout the annals of history, from a sometimes violent warrior, adventurer and industrialist to a modern seeker of status, power and riches, though instead of a male who has taken off his mothers mantel to go out in the world, we are sending out males who are still attached to their mother's breast. Society is run by adult children! Not men. Maybe this has been the legacy for the ancient masculine too? Additionally, this could be the root of the problem?

Resolution or Problem?

How does the divine masculine mature and integrate his loss and disconnection? After all, the shadow side of the male has held the reigns of power for so long. Is it now too ingrained within his male psyche, to be repaired and to evolve? The current answer to the problem, begins at a shallow level of repair, with men's groups and warrior weekends, offered to the male, places they can go to complain about how they are treated by their women, or they can revert to their inner warrior selves, adorned with face paint and reenactments of the essential warrior, who is primal and fierce, one who makes fire and sits around it in his inherent masculinity? Or he can attend counselling and psychotherapy, to talk about his feelings, and to talk about how he was hurt so badly by a prominent adult. None of this, I am decrying as it is a crucial part of trying to make sense of all the madness. However, how can the masculine find the route towards divine direction?

How can he safely adopt the role of protector, though this time one who can fight the good fight and one who imbues his spiritual strength within his core?

The Divine Masculine and a Complement of Differences

The divine masculine not only is he consort and captain, but he is also the protector of the voiceless, and he is resilient. He is one part of unity consciousness, where between the male and the female together they team up to help create a new paradigm, the golden age.

There are differences between the masculine and feminine? Well, I agree I am stating the obvious. Likewise, this has become a further part of the problem of the perception between understanding the masculine and feminine, between themselves. Because in many a household and commonly involving the younger generation who are in relationships. They expect so much more from each other. The women, want their men to show their feelings and to take regular care of their offspring. Men are expected to shop, cook and clean the home. Women want equality in socialising and in work environments. The men expect their women to be restaurant quality chefs, share the household incomes, manage the household finances and be the hottest lovers in the bedroom. These perceptions are separate from the amount of pressure each puts on themselves, to look good, buy the best clothes and to have the show home type of house to live in and to show off to their friends. Pressures are at a boiling point between the sexes, let alone the disparity in understanding who and what we are, absent of any gender separateness. Now we see terms like binary and gender fluid taking over the centre stage, we can no longer use any pronouns which differentiate gender, like him and her, male and female, Having now entered the age where gender doesn't want to exist any longer, It is becoming extinct along with masculinity and feminity, the perfect picture has changed, and it is confusing.

A Compliment of Differences

Let us keep this as simple as possible to avoid any confusion with the new definitions of human. To do this, I shall revert to the simplicity of masculine and feminine. Separate indifference by gender and biology. The male and the female, even when in divine partnership, will never be the same. It stands to reason to understand this, because males and females, think, act, desire and need different things. Though the main difference involves not only their physiology but the way each other's brains are wired. There is, of course, a reason for this, and it lies in the Creators Divine plan and how it should be executed. Due to the differences, we should ensure neither is judged or belittled. Instead, they should be celebrated as it provides both to bring the necessary ingredients to the divine purpose. We are built, and we think differently for a reason, and this is the fundamental basis to ensure we compliment the other. Because when we step back and do this, by letting go and pushing forward a need to clone our mate like ourselves. Then we assume the energetic synthesis of harmony, balance, respect and completion. To be in this state, allows the alchemical magic of architecture and creation to flow through us. We are working wholly as opposites, yet complementary to the Divines purpose for us as humans. It is okay to let your partner take time to figure out who he or she is. It's a great gift to hold space for the other, during this time also. As we tentatively approach the Golden Age, let us do so in the purest of states as humanly possible. Let us drop the roles of expectations, labels and the need for perfection in body and mind. Instead, let us find fulfilment in a relationship and work together for a common goal, one absent of all material greed and unsated desires.

Nurturing the Divine Masculine

The masculine needs to grow the seeds inside himself so that he can find his hero. He also needs to cultivate himself, during this expedition of realigning his essential self to his quintessential hero. These internal seeds should also heal the ancestral bloodlines, which, painstakingly partook in events and actions, which were violent. Man's violence must become transformed to be utilised as the energy put towards fighting the good fight. It isn't energy driven by blood lust or the synergy of greed and lust. It is energy that sustains and fervours the divine purpose and plan.

What Are the Primary Steps Now?

- Man needs to gain control of his mind, and he cannot let it become judgemental or opinionated. It is the type of energy that causes chaos and distorts the facts. His mind creates a need to defend and to be in defence of his self, and it furthers the need to gain justice and to be seen as being right and just.

- Man's speech should be tempered to create illumination and wisdom. It should not be warlike, but instead, compassionate and diverse in its dialect and understanding of other cultures and social abilities.

- A man should find the truth inside himself before sharing the truth outwardly. Truth is light, and light is purity. The truth lies in the deepest mysteries of Earth and the Universe. Therefore man should seek to discover the truth and use it as wisdom.

- Man needs to uncover every wound, trauma and insecurity and to release all feelings of lack and ability. So he can fully step into his divine self, not withheld by desires to self-medicate and greed.

- Man's life should have both meaning and purpose, not in the old ways of status and reward. But in the means of furthering man's co-creative existence with the Mother (Pachamama), the Oceans and the stars. He should open himself to other beings who exist in the unseen worlds, and he should learn how to appease, pacify and make right an imbalance.

- Man needs to nourish the Divine spark within himself, and it is the light of life and the essence of all nature.

Together with the Divine masculine and feminine release, the need to oppose the other, as the organic complement of differences, they are diverse in their expressions and experiences. And should, therefore, strive to assist one another through emotional support, unconditional love and understanding. Females should allow the male to be her protector and to captain their ship, and she should trust his direction and therefore will enable him to steer them to its end. Males should allow women to use their intuition to be able to generate the necessary energy to weave their future. She is the pregnant aspect full of possibility and the ability to make all things manifest.

It is time to allow the masculine to heal his wounds and to enter into the cave to do so. Together they can heal and release their traumas and through transparency, find their truths, and then they can both act from an authentic space. Both the Divine Masculine and Divine Feminine require acknowledgement.

Chapter 16

Dimensions and Spheres of Possibility

I'd like to introduce this section on Spheres, Energy and Dimensions to clarify and illustrate with examples, the information contained in a somewhat minefield of science, yet in its purest form, it can help us effect change for ourselves and the planet, via entering the spheres available to us.

For the majority of the un-enlightened, there is a myth held here on earth. Believed by thousands of people on the planet today, who think we are the only two-legged organisms present in the vastness of the Multi-Universes! A bold and logical belief as it is a fact apparent because there isn't any evidence to convince them otherwise. If you cannot see it, then surely it cannot exist, true or false? Okay, let us have some fun with this one. Can you see the air you breathe? It must be present. Otherwise, we would all perish. Or, you remember the virus you caught, yes that's right the one which placed you in your bed with a high fever, aches and pains and a banging headache for a week? "Yes?" Well, it's only an illusion, because did you see it attack you? Here's the last example. When you pray, or you go to the graveside to visit your loved one? And you chat away, to the grave, who are you talking too? Or when you do pray can you see who it is, you are talking to? You may intend to speak to Jesus or God, of course, yet do you see them? No? Yet we all happily pray to an unseen benevolent being.

These examples offer explanations of the everyday things we do and experience, sometimes without thought. Yet we are already traversing the aether and energy spaces to find solace or even catch mystery illnesses. But it does prove, just because we cannot see something, then it doesn't mean it doesn't exist.

Understanding Frequency

The Planet, Universe, Mother Nature, Benevolent beings, Ghosts, Spirits and Animals. All vibrate using varying forms of frequency, a mixture of positive and negative electromagnetic pulses. How much depends on each one's degree of which is paramount to its current state of resonance. Each organism, whether it is a microcosm or macronism, emits a pulse, one picked up by a similar receptacle equal to or more than in frequency. A frequency at its highest will be preceded by an ever decreasing spectrum of lower frequencies. To further explain, If we interpret a Divine being our Creator, for example, as vibrating at the fastest possible rate of incidence. Then we would expect the opposite end of this polarity to be a much slower and denser frequency. The gentler the wavelength of emission, then energy, becomes far thicker and manifests into lower physical matter. The opposite end of the scale vibrates at rates far exceeding anything reasonable and creates a form at will. The material plane (third dimension) is comprised of different vibrational atoms. For example, if you spin an object around fast enough, we would not be able to see its original form and shape.

Even our thoughts and emotions and desires vibrate at different rates. Each one attracts similar experiences of matching vibrations.

Understanding Living Energy?

Energy moves, it ebbs and flows and is continually changing returning and evolving, poignant in its rhythm. Every living thing has a pulse beating to its heart's rate. We are like a pendulum swinging back and forth, never still, never stagnant as there is always motion. Energy is vibrational, and the frequency of our vibrations are affected by many elements, these include factors from the environment, nature, emotions, other people, and thought-forms.

How you and I live, think, react, love, work, get sick and heal, is a marvellous collaboration of energy at its most effective. Whether we are exhibiting rates of emotive, positive or negativity, it all creates energy that affects not only ourselves but others and the world around us, extending like a tentacle far out into the cosmos; we are indeed a human transmitter.

Thanks to our science lessons at school, we all have a basic understanding of our bodies and how they contain 70% water. As fascinating as we find water, we know that water is never still, even if it seems motionless on the surface. We are also a composite mixture of several organising principles: oxygen, carbon, hydrogen, nitrogen, calcium, and phosphorus; these next to water, oxygen, and carbon make up the lion's share of our bodies' composition.

Philosophy determines we are a unique mixture of five platonic solids, as revealed by Plato and many other philosophers. Plato believed we embrace a set of classical elements, this being the principle that everything consists of and is based on a natural observation of matter. These five solids are: Earth, Air, Water and Fire, a fifth element was added later by Aristotle, and this was Aether or the Void. As laid out in an earlier chapter His reasoning being, the first four elements were earthly and therefore corruptible, and since there were no changes perceived in the heavenly regions of the cosmos, namely the stars, they, therefore, must be made of a different unchanging more heavenly substance, hence the fifth element. The Ancients knew each of these classic elements was fundamental to reason their primary existences.

In Egypt, the God Thoth in his form as Hermes Trismegistus attributed each element formed the basis of every living thing. For example, whether animal, insect, mineral or human, some were made of one part and others a combination. Interestingly he exhibited that some beings were more akin to the air (those that could fly); to water (those that made their homes in the oceans and rivers); to earth (those including humans who made their homes on land); and to fire (more akin to minerals). He concluded that each soul's body is weighted and therefore constricted by these four elements.

The Hindus believe all of creation, including the human body, is made up of the five elements. Upon death, the human body dissolves back to its original state, and this completes and balances the natural cycle. In ancient Tibetan philosophy, these five elemental processes are the essential materials of all existence; including emotions, temperaments, the five senses, colours, tastes and body types. They also form the basis of the calendar, astrology, and medicine, as well as the spiritual traditions of shamanism and tantra. An amalgamation of these elements and solids when placed into motion by the organising principles, not only make up our human physiology but also create a further belief, and this is the one we have trouble getting our heads around, the principle of energy.

Energy is an active component of electromagnetic particles that runs through all things. Whether these objects are seemingly motionless or termed as beings with motion. Everything we see, feel or touch is alive, the only difference being and it is what sets us slightly apart, is that it all boils down to the fact of 'differing rates of emitting frequency'. A theory that is the same for a mountain or ocean, an animal or a human, everything connects to a more significant web and reverberates. Everything links by a mixture of individual elements and solids; everything emits a rate of frequency and is therefore very much part of a network of existence.

Dimensions and the Differing States of Reality

Having discussed energy and frequency and understanding how energy vibrates at differing rates of speed. We can appreciate how solid something is, therefore, vibrating at a much slower pace of vibration. Energy is alive, and pulses throughout all things.

Everything in and out of existence has an energetic power to it at some level. If there are higher rates of energy vibrating than what we see, then these energies must exist in a different zone or space than us.

Spheres, Planes and Dimensions

We identify these spaces as spheres, planes or dimensions. Whether these planes have similarities while vibrating at differing degrees? Is unproven. Yet we can describe it as having a different state of consciousness, and this means its awareness exceeds its vibrating state of energy. We all agree we are here on planet earth now we reside within the third dimension. This dimension vibrates slower than say the space where The Divine Creator exists. The third dimension is a space held in its state by sets of human-made laws, rigid beliefs, rules for morality, and we are limited by our form. As we live, we experience our past and future is held in place by our ability to think and to feel. The third dimension is a sphere created on the principle of linear time. This time runs in a straight line from birth to death. The problem is with having such a self-imposed limitation, due to an occurring set of beliefs. We create a loop in time by assuming this as a possible experience, as the past becomes a place we focus our attention towards and in doing so, we project the same energy towards the future.

These factors alone mean we need to change our current state of belief if we want to improve our future and have the ability to dream a new world into being. First, we must change the linear way we 'loop time', towards accepting a whole new set of beliefs and abilities, which in turn open doorways to an idea in everything is possible. These new beliefs then adopt the principle of manifestation or co-creation.

To move into a higher state of consciousness requires us to change our frequency.

As mentioned previously, all energy enters into our awareness, on a like for like basis. Therefore what we think and feel is sent out and attracts a similar rate of vibration. For example, if we emit sadness, then we invite the same feeling back towards ourselves in the form of other people's grief. By setting a point of reference within our energy field, sadness is recognised, using the mirror principle of attraction, external episodes of sorrow enters and encounters a reference point. Being creatures of limitation and structure, the energy we have attracted, added to our own becomes fixed and therefore creates a more significant expression of the initial feeling of sadness. By adopting the 'time loop' principle, we have ensured that sorrow is an experience we encounter over and over again until we learn how to stop emitting its frequency.

To change this as a limiting belief, then we need to heighten our vibration and transform this energy via our hearts and in turn, changes the way we think and react. Energy cannot be dissolved only converted. When we use our ability to save energetic power, we shift our consciousness to a higher level. The goal is to head towards the fourth or fifth dimension, Spaces where we exist much more in the present time, rather than in the past or into the future. To be in current time affords us an ability to choose, and from this standpoint, we allow our consciousness and attention to become present. Observing events using a sense of detachment and allowing ourselves to 'consider' the information present and how to move forward. Rather than pulling from old experiences and outcomes to decide how an event plays out.

To recap, if we view the third dimension as a playground, where we practice understanding vibration at the level of thought, feeling and outcome from here. We also acknowledge how we come with a lot of emotional and mental baggage while existing in a third-dimensional sphere. For that reason and to move into an area of higher consciousness, for example, the fourth or fifth dimension. We must adopt a practice of emitting a higher rate of frequency in our present time, not only by making different choices but by jumping into higher consciousness. The transformation comes from moving our awareness into an altered state of perception. It is here we truly begin to understand how to dream a new land into manifestation. Choices allow us the ability to direct our will towards a required outcome, as we heighten the vibration towards a more evident capacity to transform and receive.

Understanding the Higher Dimensions

As humans, having more knowledge of the third and fourth dimensions as a differing sphere can help us with our healing. Though, how do we learn more about the higher fields and differing states of consciousness within these dimensions?

The esoteric books tell us there are 12 dimensions in all and within these are three further great planes subdivided into seven minor planes. Divided into seven subplanes that all shade into each other. Though in essence there must be so many more than we know and I was shown by a reliable source that there are 22 different dimensions in the centre of the Earth alone? Try not to think of spheres or dimensions as being stacked on top of each other like a high-rise block of flats. Remember, differing vibrating rates do not have rigid boxed in lines of definition. To envision it better, look at it as the example given in the pictorial 'Flower of Life' a sacred geometry depiction of how spheres are viewed.

I have used this symbol merely as a visual reference to see dimensions and fields differently. However, the true meaning of this symbol has layers of explanation if you research it. From containing the ancient mysteries of our existence from Adman Kadmon to, withholding the seeds and eggs of life. To encompassing the five platonic solids and being a vehicle to enter the portals into other dimensions.

Within these planes are contained all forms of material things, other forces, and manifestations of energy. Here we understand the principle of the statement 'As above, so below'. As all planes are operating at the same time, the world of spirit and matter are two different poles of the same.

[13]The Twelve Dimensions Explained

The Twelfth Dimension, the place of 'Divinity', 'The All That Is'. a consciousness of infinity.

The Eleventh Dimension, space where 'The All', manifests into 'material' to be able to create universes from a seed of positive and negative energies.

---

[13] Illuninology/Tumblr

The Tenth Dimension, the outer shell of the universe, cosmic or Christ-consciousness and other ascended conscious beings.

The Ninth Dimension, where homogenised energy takes a form like planets, galaxies, universes, stellar bodies.

The Eighth Dimension, where a group of conscious entities or group soul works together as one unit.

The Seventh Dimension, Living Vortexes, a group of beings who come in many forms, from swirling ribbons of rainbow energy to beautiful white webs of radiant light. A level that does not live on planets but rather in an intense field of the coloured atmosphere.

The Sixth Dimension, A Teaching dimension of symbols, all language, symbols, and models start here. It is where the Universe pours the archetypical moulds. At this level, we find the cast for astrological and genetic codes. It also houses the Akashic records, the complete files on everyone and everything.

This exciting dimension is a honeycomb of aspects within aspects within aspects. You could spend many long lifetimes here and never for a moment, become bored. The inhabitants are astute, quick, and exciting.

The Fifth Dimension, Heaven, or the plane of light, is the highest level a soul can reach. We incarnate here as cosmic androgynous beings. Living on stars, we don luminous Light Bodies. These eternal forms do not require pain; the warning signals that physical bodies provide.

The Fourth Dimension, the Astral plane, The Fourth Dimension is a grey, polarised plain, housing the forces of Light and Darkness. The battle between good and evil starts here. Christ was sharing a fourth-dimensional perspective when He said, "If you are not with me, you are against me." Forms naturally morph on the Astral plane. For example, a tree can quickly transform into a wolf. Because the illusion of good and evil is manifest here and because of the extreme mutability of form, distrust and fear exist.

Consequently, the strength of Personal Will or Personal Power plays a significant role in the protection and control rackets. ("I am strong and knowledgeable. I will protect and guide you and give you what you want. Just do what I say.") Magic, time travel, karma, reincarnation, luck, psychic surgery, flying, mind-reading, disembodied spirits, enchantment, and of course, astral travel, all sourced from this plane. The God(s) and Goddess(es) of many religions live here. Hell, and Purgatory is fourth-dimensional locales, as well. By embodying the principles of this plane, we enhance the probability of living a magical life.

The Fourth Dimension itself is also a honeycomb of 23 other inner spheres or spaces Guarded by a gatekeeper, and there are many avenues into other realms via this dimension.

The Third Dimension, where energy congeals into a dark, dense pool of matter. Our ability to experience beauty down here shows that we live in a loving universe. Because of the perceptual filters available (courtesy of the Planetary Consciousness), Our consciousness can identify with the matter. We can, therefore, become dense ourselves.

Because the universe allows the illusion of Free Will on the Third and Fourth Dimensions, we can act like saints or demons, or usually, somewhere in between. When we base our actions exclusively on third-dimensional principles, we live in a material world.

The Second Dimension, Biological, Second-dimensional consciousness, is an awareness on a biological level. Here you can connect with the plant and animal kingdoms. It is the consciousness that directs the autonomic nervous system to regulate and maintain life support functions. Our five physical senses are unconscious of this. The place of the chemical beings that makes up the body. You on this level can become aware of how your body is one big communication network between all the elements within your cells.

Many different beings exist on this level. Fairies, devas, nature spirits, chemical beings, elementals, and denser energies. The creation Dragons relate to on this level.

The First Dimension is the consciousness of Gaia's physical prime atom. This dimension is the realm of the mineral kingdom. Humans' first-dimensional consciousness is 'unconscious' to our five physical senses. The first-dimension part of our bodies is the minerals, water, and genetic codes that are the foundation of our physical forms. When we connect with this level, we connect with the entire physical world on a molecule level. The place of quantum physics comprises electrons, protons, nuclei, and quarks. It is the gateway between the macrocosm and the microcosm.

Shape

Dimensions should be viewed not as levels that are placed one on top of the other. Instead, consider them as vibrating forces that almost wrap around an egg-like structure that is a spiralling force. The outer layer being where the denser vibrations of Dimension 1 are, coming inwards to the centre where dimension 12 would be. In the centre is where the Divine creative force resides, massive and expansive energy that orchestrates all the other aspects.

A map of the dimensions could be viewed as a matrix.

Perception

We have a fashioned an architectural view of our reality. For all of us, evolving souls would find it easier to expand a conscious understanding of energy and how energy changes and reconfigures into either form or formless structure of its composition.

However, for some, it is harder to expand a limited set of beliefs to accept this as a possibility. Rigid beliefs create the linear way of thinking mentioned earlier and an unacceptance in all which is otherwise possible. Critical thinking can often be a driving force for individual souls who have closed down their approach to blue-sky thinking. Their perception regarding the peripheral reason and overly analysed thoughts need to escape the rigidity of ' a 3D box' Often with no fault of the self, and such possible thinking has become locked behind a closed door. Mainly due to how they have been brought up and the experiences they have had along the way. Of course, this doesn't matter, because until we all pass over from this reality to the next, perhaps 'all will become clearer'.

Some have already experienced other realms or dimensions, certainly in near-death experiences (NDE) and some lucky enough to experience them in their everyday life. Belief, knowledge and perception of the unseen realms, is attained via a nearly calcified pineal gland and the experiences reside inside our hearts. It becomes the basis and the essence of one's belief system or our inner faith; that propels most of us through life. Along with a broader ability to accept something other than what the eye sees in front.

These energies of different forces are accessible to us in our periphery visions; Noticed independently in a moment where an unusual movement of shape or colour is witnessed, glimpsed yet not caught as a held attention. Sometimes the thought of what we see can become lost in an inner expression of fear that overrides the magic of what has happened, cutting off the ability to accept all magical possibility.

Dreams

Everyone dreams, maybe not all the time, but we do, every night when we fall asleep and enter that REM phase of sleep. During this phase, we introduce a deep, yet sometimes unexplainable world of pictures, events and moving pieces. Dreams can take us on incredulous journeys and into some slightly scary outposts of our minds expansiveness. The thing is we all readily accept this otherworld, housed in our subconscious beings as usual. Often regaling the tales of sleep-time to all who will listen. Some buy books on dream interpretation and meanings, often discovering that the symbols and architecture of a dream state, provides some much-needed insights into daily life.

How can you clearly explain the places and people you meet during dream time?

Dream interpretation is more in-depth than one may think. As there are two different types of collective dream themes. One can be defined as '**Real Dreams**' and the other '**Subconscious Dreams**'. The latter a subconscious dream arises from concealed and underlying desires, often unrealised and hidden deep in our psyche. These dreams can also create obsessive behaviours or fears. On the other hand, a real dream comes as a message straight from our consciousness and when it arrives in our awareness, it provides us with knowledge or wisdom or even a prophetic experience.

The dream condition can also contain instances from previous lifetimes. Especially when the events from these lives seek out a need for justice, clemency or even require forgiveness. Let me explain and illustrate this in more detail. The many lifetimes we have experienced in human form, have set up instances and causes over time. Whatever the reason and subsequent effects arising from the root, have become images or distortions of its original state. All of these have become recorded in our soul records.

In the same way, the people who follow a mystical path seem to have more distorted dreams than perhaps someone who does not. The reason for this is a spiritual student, strives to clear his/her ideas of reality, finding the material plane limiting. Therefore when they dream they may experience the subconscious urge to clear away possible experiences and fears built from past life experiences.

Furthermore, an essential point to make here is to recognise how we find ourselves in a specific condition of life today as a consequence of being tethered to our imagination and the perceptions we create from this life. In doing so, we have become tethered to our conscious state of reality. This tethering serves only to limit our ability from being able to move freely to a higher state of frequency, and we may be able to do so in short bursts but are unable to maintain it. Merely because we are ultimately limited by fixation to our perceptive ideas.

When we enter into a dream condition as we sleep, we experience lots of dreams involving associations with other people. In this space, we are doing things we sometimes like and even dislike, and these include the things we hide in waking life, such as our fears or desires.

There are some schools of thought who say when we dream we are coursing throughout the astral plane and therefore it is here we experience astral experiences, especially when we are dreaming. Consequently, this would infer a belief in the astral plane being a place of negative experience. However, during our dream state, we do not head into the astral plane, as the astral plane is a harmonious place, devoid of repulsive experience. Here is where we can glean a better understanding of the fourth dimension and how this impacts our dream condition. There is a borderline between the third and fourth dimensions, similar to border control. When we dream, we enter into the borderline space and not the astral plane. It is a place detached from reality but infused by our contrary, repressed desires, complex fears and phobias.

The dreams we experience while in the borderland, become amplifications of the causes previously set up in this or past lives, The effects of these causes become the repressed and abandoned fears, which are present until justice, clemency or forgiveness has been attained. More importantly, understanding the reality of Dreamtime, is to recognise the importance of uncleared karma. Especially as it is our soul's conscious record of all past lives, who urges us to clear and heal our karmic load, offering us the opportunity to find a karmic reward in our lives. The soul communicates to us every night, by way of imagery, dreams, and signs and symbols. Offering us a chance to move forward into the pure light, rather than remain in a constant round of negative dream state experiences.

To conclude, this depends on our belief systems and our complex framework of ability to accept. Which seems for so many people has become hampered by the effects from a significant age in childhood, whereby sadly the belief system has become shut down or closed off by either experience, an influential adult, society or by adopting the beliefs of religious dogma.

Chapter 17

Reincarnation from the Same Branch

As you have coursed throughout the pages of this book, having delved into the woes of feminity and how we have lost so much essence from our soul records along our evolutionary pathway, owing to the gender-based racism of the patriarchal uprisings. And we have experienced how our bloodline ancestry is significant to who we are today and how much our congested karmic rivers need to be dredged and cleared. There are further matters to include and these are no necessarily gender based yet affect us all. The mystics always tell us about how the number three is indeed a sacred symbolic number. This is proven with three being representative of the Trilogy, to time being divided into three parts, the past, the present and the future. We have always seen the symbology of the three spirals of Maiden, Mother and Crone, we can ascertain how important number three is as a significant number within the cosmology of the world.

The number three shows us there are three hindrances to human evolution, these being.

1. A lack of endeavour to obtain knowledge
2. A non-attachment to Divinity
3. An attachment to Evil or darker powers

These three alone interrupt and inhibit our abilities to become mystics ourselves and to use the powers available to them, via spiritual alchemy. The first of these, which details a lack of endeavour to obtain knowledge, infers we are lazy in researching not only natural laws and facts about life but more importantly knowledge about Divine truth and wisdom. Somehow we are not able to acquaint ourselves in this pursuit. Perhaps it is because we have experienced a non-attachment to Divinity? Has this arrived from our archetypal exorcism from the Garden of Eden?, or is it because we feel we humans are self-important and have no need for a Divine Father or Mother? Maybe it's feasible to assume we have become more attached to the darker powers and enticements offered to us by the 'Dark Brothers'. All of which merely serve to keep us out of the light and engrossed in self-aggrandisement of flesh and addictive pursuits. It leads me to ask a question about how many of us are procrastinating in our spiritual exploration? How many feel they are too wounded to behold a belief or faith in Divinity? And how many have crossed the borderlands over to the dark side?

To obtain a chance to bask in the pure light of grace and wonder, we also need to appreciate there are three paths available for any individual soul.

1. Man
2. Liberty
3. Light

These paths take us from human existence and in experiencing earth lives to becoming free from the bondage of earth, via clearing our karmic rivers and freeing oneself from the need for justice, clemency and resolution, and understand the importance of forgiveness, this includes forgiving all things we have done to nature, other people and to ourselves. How can we enter into the light and adopt a merciful life, if we are hellbent on obtaining justice for one misdemeanour or another? Especially when we are focussed on gaining resolution for something terrible which befell us. Again the light awaits us and is shining brightly like the ever-present lighthouse beacon. We are offered every chance to see it and obtain the gifts from the truths it provides, even when truthfulness is buried in the alchemical geometries of symbolism and synchronicity. Conversely, this in itself becomes a hindrance because many are closed off from not only noticing the help attained from metaphors, nonetheless so often marred with the enticements from the dark.

Magic

There has long been a fight between both the dark and light and it has become famously encapsulated in the Marvel comic books adaptations affirming these battles. Put on display at the IMAX screens at the cinemas. The often impenetrable fight between the supercharged and powerful villain, often characterised as adorning horns aloft his head, or with the all-powerful and inexhaustible evil witch or long forgotten and vanquished Egyptian Goddess. She rose from her steely encased captivity, awash with boundless energy gushing from her hands. To the hero, a latex suited man or woman who often lose each ensuing battle and falls prey to these unlimited powers, until everything begins to change as humanity pulls together, and all the superheroes become a team. They can finally find enough energy to eradicate the villain.

Truthfully and this fight between the spectrums still occurs, habitually originating from specific individuals who delve into the realms of black magic, either purposely or irresponsibly. Frequently black arts and black rites involve an invocation of a dark God or Goddess, as the invocation weaves the words of power to call for assistance from the unseen. However, one can become assured that a probable invocation would invoke the 'dark brothers'. These shadowy beings who come and go at will are often unseen, due to their mysterious nature and can reach in and enter our dreams. Especially those which contain our latent fears and phobias becoming transparent as we dally on the borderlands. They wait for us to sleep because there is a sense of 'open season' as we become fair game.

People often assume they do not have control over their dream states. They feel it is a state solely governed by our unconscious minds, and many may believe dreams are not real anyway. Therefore they cannot harm you. Yet to answer this naivety, is to share, how dreams inform us in waking life, especially a particularly complex and heavy or fearful one. The energy leaves us with on waking is something we carry around all day and sometimes for days on end. Unable to shift it like a soporific stupor or lousy hangover. As soon as the dream infiltrations have finished and have left behind their distortions within our psyche. We are being manipulated from this point, as we continue with our day to day lives, having no idea with are being influenced and puppeteered by our latent fears and desires.

To follow the path of the light is often a rocky and challenging road, leading up a grim and steep mountain, one we must climb. Honestly, this is enough of a challenge for someone on the mystical path, let alone for someone who has little awareness of what is happening.

All, who have the slightest inclination of awareness, must carry with them an armoury of secret weapons, when faced with this specific type of dark energy. Even when we enter into our dream-times, we should remember reality is absent in the borderland between the third and fourth dimensions. In this grey area of wasteland, we can all become easily shaken and stirred by our repressed desires and complexes. It is here the real work begins for the metaphysical student as in ascertaining what is real and what is unreal, even though the danger here comes in a realisation that a channel has opened and has materialised from their thought expressions and therefore became a reality for themselves. How this is achieved is by knowing everything about ourselves, involving the good, the bad and downright ugly. It also comes when we are vigilant in our awareness of what we are shown in the borderland too.

Understanding Reincarnation

By understanding the simplicity and beauty of reincarnation will offer a beacon of hope and understanding of the process of living, leaving and returning from life to life. To allow the mind to stretch into a reasonable belief or notion that it is highly probable, we come back and experience many different lifetimes. Not necessary one after the other, as there would be a lot of time spent recapitulating about the experiences of the life we have just left. Nonetheless, even the thought of possible reincarnating seems to smooth out so much fear and obsessiveness of living well, when we understand a plain fact, and it is merely to share that this life is only one of many lives you will live. An equally important point to mention in this belief is to help appreciate how crucial karmic accumulation becomes. Especially as we now know Karma is carried throughout our soul's records if it hasn't been cleared, resolved or healed. While we are living, we should be mindful of embodying the teachings of acceptance as shared by the belief of the Hindus, Sikhs and Buddhists, when they say,

"Either karma can have its existence in a lifetime or dharma (Destiny) can be in existence."

There are two distinct meanings of the word dharma. The explanation is changed by using either a capital letter D or it is in lowercase. When we see Dharma in its capitalised form, then it means the 'Teachings of Buddha' if it is written as dharma and in lowercase then it infers 'A cosmic law and order are at play', as in 'It is the ways things are' or it is underlyingly governed by the 'Laws of Nature', coming into existence. If someone passes from this life with karmic accumulation, then rebirth is available for their soul. Contrary to this is if someone dies in Dharma, then resurrection does not happen again.

There was an idea, and this was active not so long ago about reincarnation being a myth, one wholly believed by many Scientists.

However, times have changed, and now proof succeeds this as many credible scientists, accept it as a possibility. We cannot deny either, how many people, including children, have such unprecedented memories of living before and being able to offer such minute and unquestionable proof of this.

Reincarnation isn't a death, it is a change in state. Of course, the body dies as it is a living organism and therefore cannot move out from the third dimension, it becomes rooted and dies by its limitation. Hence the change in the state comes from living in physical form to residing in non-physical form. As we leave this dimension through the portal into space within the fourth dimension. And unless there is a requirement to come back and rebirth the soul once more, then we move from the third dimension into the fourth, spending time with loved ones and going through the recapitulation process, until we finally go home to another sphere. Rebirth, ensures we return lifetime after lifetime until we Master the death process.

The best way I saw to explain how the process of reincarnation occurs, was explained to me like this.

Reincarnation is like a tree (perhaps the tree of life). Its branches stretch upwards and out into the cosmos, and when it is time for new life to be drawn from out of the cosmic consciousness, then the branches start to bud and flower. As the tree's buds burst into flower, the bees and insects begin the process of propagation. It is why people describe the beginning of life by the analogy of 'the season of Spring-time, as it is here we are birthed, and we start our lives, young and subtle and full of possibility. Then as we grow like the tree's leaves begin to unfurl and open, we head into 'the season of Summer', an animated and explorative aspect of the self and an excellent time for some people and a problematic hot Summer for others. As we age, our gait slows, and we begin to look back over our lives, we head into our Autumn years, and our life force withers slowly, then as the physical form wears out and when we die, the leaf finally falls from the tree of life to the floor.

Eventually, the leaf dries out even more, and it becomes battered by the wind and the rain, and the moisture from the elements, helps the leaf feedback into the roots around the tree of life. Here it remains, waiting for a chance to rebirth itself and in this cycle of reincarnation, the spring comes around once more, and we see new leaves growing on the very same tree, awaiting their chance to live again. Within this cycle is an analogy there is a science of perfect law and order at play here, managed by the universe and its endemic Laws of Nature. Therefore nothing exists or lives without first following the Law of Nature and its Universal natural phenomena. Yet many forget to read the small print with appertains to these laws, which says,

"By learning from the mistakes of the past, we learn not to repeat the same in the present."

Chapter 18
We Are the Mysteries!

All indigenous faiths were derived from their 'first people' meaning those who first came to earth. The mysteries are rooted in the pasts of these initial human pioneers. When they arrived, they arrived without any sort of pre-ordained sets of religious texts and books. Their religion (for want of a better word) came from what they experienced, and it is these experiences that have become rooted in the purity of the past. Africa is the seat of the first human incarnation, and it was these inhabitants who became the early ancestral traditions, from which those who succeeded them followed. The ancestors were the first line of defence in a very uninhabited world. What these first ancestors left their progeny was a sacred knowledge that was expressed through what is termed as binary oracles, these showed the way and became the basis of mathematics, ecology, biology and community.

A binary oracle is a written text or symbolism often in the form of divination, designed to open portals for the God/esses to speak through.

The early ancients indeed achieved great feats in architecture. These can be seen today in their capability of building, unusual structures, as in the stone circles, tombs and early temples as well as the pyramids. Each structure's fabric held within it the patterns of the cosmos and reveals how those early societies based themselves around the Natural laws, the sun, the moon cycles, the planets, star constellations and astrological systems. It was embedded within the peoples' spirits how all the laws of the universe are expressed through nature. They knew everything began in the vast darkness and was birthed through the cosmic womb. Early human life emanated this primary expression via its own family and belief systems. Indeed these first inhabitants understood the importance of nature and its elements. How every aspect was alive with consciousness, it was here each character was awarded deity status, worshipped and revered as the giver of life. From Mother Water who keeps us alive with vital fluids to the Mother Earth who provides us with everything, we need to Father Sun who warms our bodies and gives us fire, and the Mother Air without whom we couldn't breathe. Everything in nature had a purpose and supported us as a system of beings if we didn't have it, then we know we would not survive. Respect was afforded to each life-giving element, as well as to the Mami Wata beings who became the first teachers and way-showers. These elements were given deity status and are still today worshipped as Gods.

The destiny of humans relied intensely on an understanding of the facts about how the Cosmos, Creation and the planets and Earth itself are all interrelated and therefore, all manifestations of the first creative principle, coming from ' the Divine Creator's breath' this is where everything begins and ends. In each cycle or generation, there have always been gifted humans who can access via a connective inner, knowing the secrets of the mysteries. In ancient times it was these Priest(esses) and Medicine men and women who held rank as their powers were able to tap straight into the vital essence of the aether and otherworlds. It is why the later human-made religions became obsessed with stealing these abilities. And why it was these seemingly 'religious normal men', those who did not have the gifts passed down through their bloodlines became so flawed. It was in their greed and obsessive behaviours which urged them to murder, enslave, take and degrade the Priest(esses) as 'witch doctors', witches and sorcerers. It is why so many of us now in the twenty-first century has such an impeded view of the mysteries. As we are spiritually handicapped by the religious patterns, those who have been forced on us for millennia, wherein we too have inherited their doctrines in believing in the opposites of angels and demons and good and evil. It is also why for many, it is difficult to return to the moral purity which existed at some point in early man's existence. The patterns of religions have hidden this purity so deeply behind blockades and walls. Desperate to ensure none of us breakthrough to embody the incorruptible knowledge of the truth. Because then and only then would the walls of control come tumbling down!

What Are the Mysteries?

The mysteries are found in both truth and wisdom. They detail our route from the Divines first breath to an awareness of the many incarnations a form of a human, or another intelligent being has had via incarnating throughout the five root races. The mysteries ask us to conceive the hidden information found in those ancient texts, which reveal the secrets. Whether you examine the early binary oracles found in the Tifinagh texts, whose origins are from around the second Millenium BC, an old type of alphabet from the Tuareg people of North Africa, of which some say is closely related to the Phoenician (Eastern Mediterranean) alphabet. The Tifinagh texts are descendent of the more widely known Berber scripts. Or, the Hakata tablets of Southern Africa, or the Book of Fate from Egypt. Even to the Holy Odu, a system of divination from the Yoruba people and its sacred teachings passed down orally for thousands of years, consisting of wisdom and history set out through 256 binary codes. All of these holy texts and oracles are how the Priest(esses) imparted the mysteries to our ancient ancestors.

During the sixteenth century, a latter form of sacred script emerged and was channelled via the Angelic realms. These texts include the Malchim Script, from the Angels or messengers in Judaism to the Celestial Scripts, now also used in pagan terms, To the Enochian alphabet transmitted to Dr John Dee (1527–1608) by angels. It seems somehow more acceptable as humans evolved through the fifteenth and sixteenth centuries for the term angel or (Malakh, in Judaism) to be widely accepted as in their existence alone. However, the human-made religions soon turned artistic licence in how they portrayed an angel looked, as human-like with wings to become the norm. Rather than possibly representing the different hierarchies of Angels as having many different eyes and many wings and sides to them.

The Angelic Realm

Angels have such a lot of religious connection; they in themselves are a hive, a unique class of supernatural entities. Known as divine agents and sacred messengers, they are intermediaries between the Creator, creation, Christianity, the Kabalah and Neoplatonism.

Where they reside is everywhere and within the many higher dimensions. Some are more closely connected to Earth, others are connected to the natural elements, while others are entirely disconnected from humans and guard the thresholds between the planes of existence. If you want a better understanding of how they inhabit the different realms and spaces, take a look back to the drawing of the 'flower of life' to appreciate the closeness and interconnectedness of these planes. Angels are categorised via rays, shades of space and frequency. Yet do not be seduced by the religious view of them in humanised form as we should appreciate these beings are not human in any way at all.

Furthermore, there are indeed nine ranks of angels, and within those ranks, there are many levels and differing appearances. All have different functions and jobs. Again it would be helpful to understand how the multi-verses, galaxies, planets and the Earth plane itself, as well as the inner-Earth, all, contain many different beings and contacts. Human and animal are merely a couple of grains of sand amongst a beach full of sand.

Angels can be either creative or destructive principles, they permeate everything, and it is through their patterns of existence, which Divinity flows through, so it can manifest throughout all forms of creation. Angels form the bridges and borders between the spaces, with some providing access routes between the mundane material realm and the Divine realms.

Demons

Due to our patterning belief of a monotheistic view of the Divine, we represent the beings who are opposed to light as being separate. Whereby Angels are good, and demons are evil. Yet, they are but the other side of the same coin. All celestial beings may be either benevolent or malevolent, depending on their relationship to the Supreme Being.

On the other hand, the bible and other religious books have inferred that Demons are fallen, angels, The chief angel is Lucifer or Satan as he became more commonly known, was the primarily fallen angel who left the grace of God, after rebelling and then others followed him into the pits of hell, with a remit to promote dark deeds. Religion also tells us about how Angels reach the heights of divinity, whereas demons reach down into the greatest depths of hatred, bitterness and perversion. Again, religious doctrines want us to view this separateness as being right because it can then punish humans who choose to err on the side of sin, lust and perversion instead of righteousness and piety.

Demons are angels, who work in different ways. They are not necessarily the evil-minded dark purveyors; we may envisage. But instead, they work using methods of destruction, demons do not have a devious agenda perse, or so-called human emotions or are they trying to promote the ways of darkness and shadow, consciously or with purpose. They could care less about humans at all. Truthfully the law of polarity deems there must be energies that are opposing forces because this ensures balance can be attained within the universe. Therefore it is not about good versus evil but to some extent a necessary mix of different sides which retain and maintain balance. After all, the Divine Creator, cannot continue just to create things one after the other. There has to be a restriction in place to maintain the balance. Angels of all manifestations are the adhesive between the inner and outer realms; it is the human-made religions that should come under scrutiny and become accountable for their behaviour and actions after diminishing her story. It is humans who create the worst atrocities here on earth, and those who have committed them espousing the name of so-called divine justice have crossed the boundary into the dark side. It is Iyami, along with the Angels, who fight to ensure balance can be maintained in the aether.

Iyami Are Contained Within the Mysteries

To explain more by way of understanding who Iyami are? Is first to return to their name Iyami which means (Our Mothers), this name seeped in the African traditions, passed down from mother to child, throughout all the ages. It is explicitly linked to African etymology because this is where life was primarily seeded; it is the source of the mysteries. Yet to fully appreciate their Divine greatness let us return to the Divine Creator, as he breathed life from out of the void, Iyami are his children, his primary progeny. Known as the galactic mothers of all, they are the Mothers of all existence, including the other Gods and Goddesses and all living things, (not just humans and animals). It is why we revere them as 'Super Goddesses'. Perhaps even this title isn't of a high enough accolade either? They are the creators of life, they sustain life, and they can destroy life. Not in a whim, nor as a punisher, yet more as being able to right any imbalance between the multi-verses, cosmos and nature.

Iyami, are known widely in the Yoruba traditions of Vodoun and Mami Wata. Though they are so much older than this, manifesting during Lemuria and Atlantis in those early root races. They are the super-powerful ones, whose powers are expressed via the elemental, biological and creative superior codes in the source of all things. They are supreme healers, and present in all destruction and physical and spiritual development. They are known as the Mother Gods in other cultures who followed on from the migrations out of Africa, as well as further seedings across the globe.

The term 'Aje' is another one of Iyami's praise names, 'Iyami Aje', this name is a Yoruba word, signifying a biological and spiritual power that is beyond all definition. A name that has since become demonised due to the incoming Abrahamic religions. As did all the gifts and skills women possessed, such as Midwife, Medicine-herbalist, Magician, Guide, Seer, etc. Yet the true term Aje means those who have lived on Earth and who are the ancestral mothers. Iyami beholds mysterious forces. She is the ultimate and primary mysterious mother.

The Route to the Divine Mysteries

The mysteries find their source outside all human-made religions. Though their legitimacy is found embodied along the path of purity and truth. They are discovered when we explore the ancient mystery teachings, and the secrets are often hard to find. As they are secreted behind the invisible veils in the places, humans cannot always get access to, or are carefully guarded away from personal impropriety. Often they have become hidden in plain sight, encoded inside all mythic tales and pictorially symbolised on the walls of tombs, temples and caves. It has been done to adequately safeguard them from getting into the hands of those who are not worthy enough to know them. These mysteries would if in the wrong hands, shed light on the very source of creation, as well as give them untapped access to all the other immaculate beings and otherworld contacts. Already many Deities have become imprisoned within temples and encased inside religious buildings throughout the patriarchy. Used for aggrandisement and to allow the human to access the inner realms and libraries. Then again, for some fortunate souls, it is written in their destiny to search and seek all which has been hidden, these are the luminous warriors in human form alive now, who have a clear dispensation to do so, the reason is to help humanity and to bring purity to the modern world.

All knowledge that is sourced from divine wisdom needs to be integrated within the luminous warriors being, and this happens purely via osmosis and inner knowingness. The teachings are sought solely from a place of purity and pulled inside the person, where activations begin to occur. The motive is to align the said light-warrior with the forces prevalent to all life. More than ever, are these ancient forces required now in the modern world, as they were and are rooted in inequality, balance and reciprocity. Now, today there is a deficit of all these qualities, there is a lack of divine justice, honouring of Mother Earth and there is mismanagement being carried out by a lot of impure souls who delve carelessly into other realms. Man has set him/herself up as a false and external shadow force of God and has become disrespectful in his actions and behaviours while doing this.

The market place a name for Earth is presided over by Iyami Aje, yet man still has little knowledge of their existence. Though their creative powers flow through everything, whether one has good health or bad health, or someone always has bad luck, this is weighed and balanced by Iyami Aje. If human beings only paused for a minute to understand how these powers permeate everything and can help anyone who seeks change. Instead of lamenting about how things continuously go wrong for them. Alternatively, they may well take a step back to explore, how these forces, who are more significant and influential than all humans, can and will intervene to help us.

It is a sad truth that humankind has forgotten how to respect and revere, all existences which he/she cannot or will not acknowledge. We have instead become a stereotypical clone of the thousands of souls throughout history who have gone before. Lost in its vanity of image. We view the mysteries along with the mystery schools, and secret societies as dangerous and with suspicion, mainly due to a lack of understanding. Though there are secret societies all over the globe and within the inner earth. Known by many names, from 'Iyambo Ekpe' in the Igbo people to the 'Matrikas' in Tibet and India, The 'Lechuzza' in Mexico and the 'Black Doves' in Europe. Iyami have been a part of these secret societies as they incarnated throughout hundreds of thousands of years. The place where the mothers gather in the inner planes and meet their children and kin during the dream states.

Today in Africa, there is a secret society of elders who are connected to Iyami known as Ogboni. It is a place highly secretive, and only those of the royal Iyami bloodline and soul group may enter.

Iyami Informs Her Kin

Some of Iyami are primarily aligned with Mother Earth, Pachamama and are expressed through the elemental forces. Governing the seasons of the earth, along with the inner workings of the planet. Other Iyami remains far more cosmic and stellar and not confined to the earth-plane or even the galaxies. It helps us all understand how they are not only cosmic or earthly but also have the ability to have interrelationships with everything in existence, whether seen or unseen.

Iyami informs her kin and her children so they can also access the primordial spirit of all creation which is her. She requires a close relationship and bond with them because they are her able and willing hands here on earth. Carrying out her will or directly being able to fulfil the destiny of making good man's previous mistakes. She expresses urgently, throughout the many facets of spirituality on the planet now and ensures transparency is revealed. As many have taken on the spiritualised mantle as Teachers, Gurus or Healers, There is for some the lack of purity, in essence, making them unable to fulfil the required mastery impeccably. Today there is a vast wave of spiritual classes and workshops, all promising enlightenment or abundance and exceptional healing abilities. Many promise ascension and a place in the golden age. More often than not, the course itself is usually either only a one day or weekend class, after which you are provided with a certificate declaring, you can heal anyone, or perhaps it ensures you a place on the next spaceship out of here when things get tough. The teachers, many of whom themselves are unhealed and can create destructive chaos within their teaching space. Subsequently, this energy can inflict itself on a vulnerable and willing student. So many Spiritual teachers today are neo-pagans, who source their knowledge from a narrow breadth of teachings, wherein they teach from the pool of wisdom which does not go beyond, the religious patterns of the Abrahamic faith system, who capped the source teachings. Though they offer classes in, Witchcraft, Druidry, Shamanism, etc., it is not necessarily sourced from the pure, unadulterated wisdom only found beyond the cap.

Onward Progress

With all that has been said, the mysteries and the inner depth of profound truth must be sought impeccably and with integrity. Not everyone can access these hidden libraries or make contact with the inner adepts or beings. However, there is a compromise and one which is open to all. The journey towards self-improvement via spiritual understanding and learning how to access all areas of the mysteries can offer the seeker much freedom from the tyranny of mind and liberation of one's soul. There are ways to achieve solace and peace alongside living your daily lives. Not only is this a gift for everyone, but in exchange, it would be respectful to acknowledge the story beyond the commonly known history books, and I hope this book will be the start of an even further search for you to undertake.

Remember the Divine Mothers Iyami are always watching how we as humans act, they are interested in our reactions and our behaviours. The requirement is to wake up and repair and clean our karmic river, and they also ask we honour our ancestors. They need us to reconnect with the natural laws which govern the universe. Though most of all, there is an importance to retain and maintain balance within your own life. Think about this Chaos invites destruction. Balance invites joy and peace.

To close here are some ways to help you to increase your relationship with Iyami and your soul's destiny.

- Make effective prayers that draw you into a sacred space where communication and exploration are attained via a request for wisdom via knowledge.
- Align with your destiny; discover your purpose here in life.
- Wisdom comes with understanding that everything continually transforms.
- Understand the life, death, and rebirth cycles.
- Find the keys to open the doors, which inhibit your healing, and dare to walk through them.
- Maintain your health, mind and body.
- Exercise caution in investigating the mysteries find only wisdom and avoid the tricks.
- Balance is attained between work, rest and play.
- Understand how personal development is an ongoing process.
- Be open-minded.
- Welcome your ancestors, explore the karma accumulated through the bloodlines and celebrate their past achievements, find out about your family's own physical and mental illnesses.

- Find ways to open the paths which you find are blocked. Calm your waves of anger, frustrations and victim mentalities. Follow the guidance of spirit and your ancestors.
- All cycles end if transformation is achieved and with proper and timely handling. A change of perception moves us forever forward.
- A connection to spirit brings forth new life, and opportunities and it is the true path to illumination and ascension.

And Finally, as of January–August 2020

Everything that is happening now, regarding the pandemic, lack of freedom and social distancing was pre-prepared by Iyami.

During this time of apparent illusion, there are two reasons for the isolation, Iyami is preparing her children and those affiliated via mixed human-Iyami marriage, to remove the human paradigm of fear, within themselves and to counsel others to do the same. It is also to allow the nervous system to calm down and the Divine Lords of Karma and justice to help clear away the accumulation of karmic sludge, found in people and on the Earth in readiness for the incoming Golden Age. They are working with people regularly to remove the imprint of fear. Especially during the night when people are asleep.

Instead of gathering and brandishing a sword to defend this earth, they are asking us to bring around us a state of equilibrium. The answer and assured route of ascension towards the Golden Age are achieved by expressing creativity in every way, whether this is done academically, reading, art or writing or by working in your kitchen. They urge us to live a wholesome life, the way it is meant to be lived in the Golden Age.

Instead of rising up with arms to take the world back from the dark forces, who are currently taking advantage of this pandemic and lockdown. They want humans to choose a wholesome life, this then stops the ego-mind from proffering a sense of false power. It should then promote our physical, mental, emotional, and spiritual bodies to be on top form as well as heightening our frequency. Though it is crucial and timely to add that the layers of residue from the extensive human paradigm, throughout it many existences must first be shed before entering the Golden Age.

They say we have in the past and up to this point, been wielding false power influenced by belief systems, whether this has come from religion, indigenous people, governments, or the dark armies. It has created a fear-based reality in those working with the light as this has created an over-dominant ego urged on by belief systems, forcing the ego to become confused. Welding power correctly means we should surrender to the will of the Divine Mothers and the Most-High and remove the ability to second guess evil.

I close this book, offering love and good health to you all.

Ashe.
Iyanla.

Appendum
A Gift from The Mothers – Iyami

Speak aloud this decree, within sacred space for seven days

This decree is to be used by all Men of all Spiritual lineages.

Please note Women can say it too if they feel called to do so.

A declaration/decree spoken to receive the sacred grace required to restore the original masculine/feminine Creation-Sequence. This must change within men of all spiritual lineages especially the Lineage Keepers on Earth now.

As many still carry the matrix of false masculinity which has been woven by the religiosity/culture after the Fall of man. It is held within mans DNA, his cells and atoms. Creating imbalance having stalled the incoming Full Grace of The Divine Mothers. This decree will remove latent toxicity and all buried shadow masculinity from within man's DNA and cells.

Opening Sacred Space

Through the law of love and through the law of grace.

In the name of the Divine Fire of Earth

Guardians of the Core of the Earth

I call forth the fifteen Dimensional Divine fire from the belly of the Mother

And the highest to touch the belly of the Mother.

Bless me in your presence.

With your love and with your sisterhood.

I call forth, the sisterhood that is imbued by the power of the Mother.

And the Divine Mother herself.

Wait until the energy comes in and PAUSE.

REPEAT 3x times.
THE DECREE

- Tap the LEFT leg powerfully on the floor/Earth (3x times).
- Say out loud.

By the Divine Decree of the Sacred Mothers-Iyami. (say 3x times).

I request the Holy Sacrament of the Iyamis, Divine Mothers.

To now fully and peacefully restore my cells and life to the original design of the Most-High/ Creation. (say 3x times).

1. Pause and feel the peace
2. Tap the RIGHT leg, powerfully on the floor/Earth (3x times)
3. Say out loud

I am now balanced in the Holy design of Original Creation on all planes of life.

Gratitude to our Iyami and the Most-High. (say 3x times)

Lastly

Purpose and History

Whether we appreciate Iyami Osorongo, in their cosmic form, or as Elder kin here on Earth they have a concise and defined purpose and primarily this is to maintain and restore balance and justice, within the heavens and cosmos and here on this planet, it is clear and straightforward. And there is a much-needed motivation for their role and action. One purely born from the tirade and chaos which remained after several invaders from incoming star races who after arriving on this planet caused a lot of instability. These star-races sought to tamper and change human DNA, as well as take precious metals out of their core; all of this occurred between 300,000 years. to 900,000 years ago. A timeline so far back, many cannot even comprehend there being intelligent life on the planet of Earth. Yet there was. The first root race now termed the 'ancient human race' was an androgynous being who were birthed by the seeds implanted by Iyami. An advanced intelligent human who communicated telepathically and could create offspring without the need of a man/women coupling. They had the birthing function within themselves, producing their children via a sac produced from their own body, which was laid within a soil nest inside the Earth. To allow the child to imbue the codes from the Earth, the cosmos, and the source of its existence.

When the Most-High or Supreme Creator begins to create a galaxy, and I'll explain why in a moment. They also develop Hierarchies of Nature Spirits who are placed within the planetary solar systems and on the stars throughout the galaxy. These Nature Spirits can be imagined as being simple to those who have an extraordinarily advanced consciousness.

The reason and purpose for the creation of a galaxy are to allow different beings from all the realms of existence to be able to have experiences in physicality. They incarnate into physical bodies or vehicles, and they come from various off planetary system star groups, consciousnesses and dimensions.

This first race lived on Earth, harmoniously for aeons, until the invading star races arrived. Back then, our Earth was vastly different, and it was lush and beautifully abundant place with rolling forests, hills and clear water.

It may be prudent to mention at this juncture, that the star races in question here, do not reside merely in the stories of science fiction. Furthermore, they have been recorded throughout the creation stories, cave paintings, cuneiform tablets, and hieroglyphics of our earliest known ancient ancestors. Notably, the African tribes of Dogon, Zulu, Akan, Ewe and Dagara. The Egyptian Old Kingdom, and the Sumerian/Babylonians, as well as in the Chinese/Korean/Japanese people of the Far East and the Indo-Europeans.

The invading star races mentioned here are the Sirian Reptilian Factions from the dog star Sirius, (termed as a masculine electricity principle) they are a race of dog/wolf beings who joined via marriage and to show loyalty to the Orion-Reptilians, (The feminine matriarchal magnetic principle). This coupling came after a failed attempt by the Sirians to invade the Orion's, and their endgame was one of do or die.

The ancient tribes of the Akan, Dogon and Zulu tell stories of a time in their history when these beings arrived, as they recount it was in a furious blaze of fire and lightning when these huge ships came suddenly from out of the sky. When they landed, the early ancient races witnessed a half-man who stood upright on two feet, he had the head of a reptile and fish skin running down its body. They said these beings needed to live in water, and the story explains how, on their arrival, they had to create vast pools of water to dive into, to survive. It is important to note here a fact born from several early civilisations who even today recount how they first came from the stars, especially Sirius and Pleiades, this includes, The Africans, Peruvians and Mayans as well as the Early Iraqi peoples of Sumeria. In truth, you would be hard pushed to find a human culture here on Earth now, who have not first had affiliations or who haven't any genetically modified DNA within them which would have formerly come from the Pleiades, Antares or Arcturus, Andromeda or the Centuri star systems as well as Sirius and Orion.

To determine why these beings came to Earth promotes a clash of theories. They have been described as the Annunaki, or the Nephilim or the Children of Enki or Sons of Anu. Some say they only came to Earth because they needed to harvest Earths precious resources, for example, to mine for gold a valuable commodity, and which is abundant mainly in South Africa and Sumeria. While others explain their reason for coming as being one merely to modify humans with their DNA and to create a semi cloned race who were malleable and could be used to fight wars and work for them, Whichever camp you fall into, there is further evidence and a better way to explain by understanding who we are as humans today.

Within human DNA, there is an unknown quantity of which scientists can confirm, especially in the African races. This hidden gene pool could have come from the Orion (Snake/Reptile) and Sirius (Dog/Wolf) coupling pools, or even from other star races, such as Draco or the Pleiades. However, it is fair to say many cultures around the globe, whether from Africa, Chinese/Korean/Japanese, or Indo-European and even the early Native Tribes. Contain an unknown DNA portion within them.

To unravel this idea further, we can see how the actions and behaviours mostly reveal this. Let me break this down also, to focus on a particular type of human whose emphasis is merely on their mind and body and the importance they give to their mental and physical attributes, these aspects are found inside the higher powers and heads of companies and governments today and even throughout and within the spiritual arena, take yoga for example. However, I am not by any means degrading yoga and its principles, only to illustrate the importance and mindset placed in the pursuit of perfection of the body and mind.

Imagery found in temples around the globe indicates further evidence to the clues relating to the source of human DNA, these range throughout the compelling images and totems of snakes/serpents, crocodiles, and turtles that became a revered totem for the early modified ancestors of our cultural lineages. The Dogons also revered the being we know as Nommos or Mami Wata, and one which previews in one of the earlier chapters of this book. You will also find in the ancient Sumerian people and the Babylonian empire who revered the Oannes, who are similar to the Nommos.

The mystery that surrounds the Sirius invasion includes not only the sub-Saharan races of Africa and of course Egypt. But also, Sumer and the Babylonian Empire, as well as non -indigenous Earth people, such as Atlantis, Lemuria, Dravidians (India), Yu/Gobi Desert (China) as well as several other planets in the solar system. The Sirian geneticists are the original builders of planetary architecture, and they are termed as being both a benevolent and a harmful race of beings. Sirius itself as a planet is in the higher dimensions. However, there are timelines throughout the history of Sirius B that became corrupted by the Orion group and its reptilian invasions. Sirius B, in its highest vibratory form, is a twenty-fourth dimensional outpost. Yet, the Sirius portion in play here is in a lower density of the sixth dimension and had access to the free-world systems.

It became known during the second seeding of humans here on Earth, how the renegades from Sirius came after being influenced by the Luciferian, Marduk races. (Marduk, is a God in Mesopotamian religion, the chief god of the city of Babylon and the national god of Babylonia). Their reason for coming to Earth and other areas in the solar system was because the Sirian Reptilian race decided they wanted to create their own host bodies.

Guardians

There is now and always has been guardians present on Earth those whose prime function was to maintain and guard the earthly portals and interdimensional portals found between the human realms and the realms of the Nature spirits and higher worlds. Even today in some tribes in Africa, this role is undertaken by queer men and women, even though they may marry and have children of their own in the same way as the other tribal members. It is these special guardians who have within them an extremely high frequency that courses throughout their being and is primarily needed to guard these portals.

The Earth and Cosmological guardians hold within them the magic of the ancient seers. While working alongside the beings/humans who maintain and guard the planet shamanically, by employing the old skills of high magic, and by working with the spirits and elements of the four directions; Air/Wind, Water/Rivers and Oceans, Earth/Body of this planet and Fire/Sun. These systems of magic and shamanism maintain balance and justice here on Earth and throughout the cosmos. Without these beings/humans who are in service solely to this work, Earth and its galaxy would be in much more considerable danger.

Genetically Modified

The genetic experiments were carried out 300,000–900,000 years ago by the Sirian-Reptilians on the first ancient humans. Produced a different type of human. One who has evolved into the modern race of global humanity we now know. For example, these geneticists came from the warrior types on Sirius who conjoined with the intelligent reptiles from Orion.

We can see this impact, throughout our semi-modern history books and none more so than in the dark ages. It is here; we fully comprehend the effect of such a rise of aggression, and the way organised religions swooped in to convert the indigenous peoples, their reason we could easily assume was to deny their divine abilities, steal the mysteries and shut down these portals. History also details a sudden global epidemic of marauding home-land invaders whose aim was to dominate and acquire other nations property.

In present-day Africa, killing, fighting and domination is a way of life. Around the world gangland, behaviour, aggression, shooting, and stabbings have become normal between rival gangs. Surely in part, it must be down to the way our DNA was hijacked.

After all, as much as we experience this darkness that runs through our societies, exhibited by the prowess behaviours of pride, egotism, arrogance, acts of brutality, wanton destruction, dominance, a need for vengeance, death and honour. All of which are attributed to the ways of the Sirian wolf/dog beings and coupled with the influential input of the Orion Reptilians who are insidious, intelligent, cunning, clever and inventive. They also poison us physically (which we now experience via our food chain and in our drinking water) and mentally (by mind control). All of this unfolds, driven by those in positions of power, especially in the areas of economics, finance, acquisition of property, technology, and science etc.

Consider how this change in DNA could birth a specific type of criminal mind, for example. Manifested specifically in the profile of evil geniuses or the criminal masterminds or the serial killer, (after all, reptilians need to hunt). It is a prime example of a prolific nature fuelled by a nurtured unknown DNA interference, and surely this makes sense as to why particular individuals choose a criminal life?

Before leaving you to ponder this research, I would like to close by explaining that it is not all doom and gloom. By illustrating how long ago our genetic tampering occurred, it was aeons ago! In saying this, we should also appreciate our gene pools can further negative or positive actions and behaviours, which explains the considerable advancement in 'Alternative Spiritual Warrior Movements'. Every human being does have a choice, and this is backed up by the gift we have of utilising free will, our decisions, actions, words, and behaviours dictate the side we choose to fight on.

The spiritual path of the spiritual warrior embodies spirit within them. Incarnated into physical form. Not only does the journey of the warrior challenge themselves via life's battles and challenges, but also via the lesser positive influences generated via genetic tampering of their DNA. The struggle continues to regain self-control and sovereignty of mind and body, absent of cultural ideals and beliefs.

The Spiritual Warriors goal is self-realisation attained via discipline and increased awareness, our journey of endless research and understanding helps us appreciate how these trials and quests, lead us towards clarity and helps us to regain personal power. It is a personal quest to seek the holy grail of purity and truth, as we find our way back to the source. Along the way, each of us discovers his/her path towards 'Spiritual Warriorship'. Culminating in the pursuit of being in-service to other humans, animals, and by caretaking Mother Earth (Pachamama). As one of my teachers, Dr Alberto Villoldo says.

"Pachamama, sweet mother, I am not part of the problem, I am part of the solution."

But the dictate of the spiritual warrior is further explained by Carlos Castaneda who said:

"A warrior is frugal and utilises every bit of his energy without wasting it.

A warrior must be fluid and shift harmoniously with the world around him.

A warrior seeks freedom and does his ultimate best to regain balance in his spirit."

And this is a prudent reminder for us all, and this story will continue.

Ase and Aho